Adventures In
Italian Cooking

*Created and
designed by
the editorial staff
of ORTHO Books*

*Written by
James McNair*

*Edited by
Annette C. Fabri*

*Book design by
James Stockton*

*Photography by
Tom Tracy*

*Photographic styling by
Sara Slavin*

Ortho Books

Publisher
Robert L. Iacopi

Editorial Director
Min S. Yee

Managing Editor
Anne Coolman

Horticultural Editor
Michael D. Smith

Production Editor
Barbara J. Ferguson

Editorial Assistant
Maureen V. Meehan

Administrative Assistant
Judith C. Pillon

Recipe Testing
and development by
Susan E. Mitchell
Carolyn E. Petersen
Alice P. Gee
Bonnie Lahti

Copyediting by
Editcetera
Berkeley, CA

Typography by
Terry Robinson & Co.
San Francisco, CA

Color Separations by
Color Tech Corp.
Redwood City, CA

Address all inquiries to:
Ortho Books
Chevron Chemical Company
Consumer Products Division
575 Market Street
San Francisco, CA 94105

1 2 3 4 5 6 7 8 9 10

Printed in August, 1980

ISBN 0-917102-89-4

Library of Congress Catalog
Card Number 80-66345

Credits and Acknowledgments

Consulting home economist
Nancy May

Consulting professional chefs,
Luciano Parolari, Executive Chef
Villa d'Este, Lake Como, Italy
Jody Purcell, San Francisco

Wine consultant
Bill Grinager

Special consultants
Jean Salvadore, Villa d'Este, Italy
Marian E. May, San Francisco
Count and Countess Crespi,
New York
Lin Cotton, San Francisco
Val and Albert Daigen, Toronto
Mona Simpson, San Francisco

Additional photography
by Picnic Productions

Props for photography

Statements, San Francisco
Jeffrey Felsen, The Catered Affair,
San Francisco
Christian Nelisen, Axiom Design,
San Francisco
Williams Sonoma, San Francisco
Hudson Bay Company, Oakland
Rattos, Oakland
Linda Hinrichs, San Francisco
Salamari, Milan

Adventures In
Italian Cooking

Italian Cooking Update 4

Time-honored cooking methods and ways of serving Italian foods are keeping pace with the sleek design of modern industrialized Italy. Yet the food remains firmly rooted in the peasant lifestyle, where emphasis is placed on fresh ingredients prepared and presented simply.

Your Italian Kitchen 10

Most cooks have on hand almost all the essential equipment to cook Italian style, but some items add authenticity and adventure, while other gadgets make kitchen chores easier. Stock up on imported or domestic ingredients and seasonings from nearby markets or via mail.

Italian Recipes 18

Our collection of recipes from Italy and Italian-American communities follows the order of the typical Italian meal. Cook as the Italians do, using the recipes as a guide but adapting them to make use of the fresh vegetables, fruits, meats, and fish that are available seasonally.

Italian Cooking Update

From Italy come some of the best-loved foods in the world. It's difficult to imagine what the American dinner table would be like without the foods brought to it by the Italians who settled here. Minestrone, spaghetti, macaroni, ravioli, and pizza now seem almost as American as apple pie. What's more, Italy has given the world such amenities of gracious dining as forks and table napkins.

For centuries Italy was divided not only by mountains, rivers, and other geographical barriers, but by often hostile political boundaries as well. Gastronomically, this resulted in the development of distinctive regional styles of cooking.

For example Bologna, in Emilia-Romagna, is the source of rich, cream-sauced foods; Florence, only an hour's train ride away, features the simplicity in preparation characteristic of Toscana. In the last century, of course, the cuisine has begun to be unified along with the nation, and a national cuisine is slowly emerging. As Italian cooking has evolved in Italy, Italian cooking in America has taken on a flavor all its own. Italian-Americans still cook Old World regional specialties, but they've added

Today's sleek look and ultraconvenient techniques are far removed from Italy's gastronomic heritage. Quick-action electric pasta machines (opposite) *are rapidly replacing time-honored methods, passed through families over the centuries, that produced handmade pastas such as these* (right) *photographed in a Venetian shop window.*

5

recipes from neighbors, friends, and relatives of different backgrounds. In so doing they have married the New World with the Old to create such original dishes as San Francisco's *cioppino* and New Orleans' *muffalata* sandwich.

Thus this book is not a collection of regionalized Italian specialties, but a compendium of the best offerings of the nation as a whole along with the adaptations and additions of Italian-American family cooking.

San Francisco's famous North Beach Italian community reflects both the traditional and updated Italian spirit. Columbus Day in Washington Square (above left) is an excuse for each family to prepare favorite foods from treasured Old World recipes.

Pasta factories (above right) turn out vast quantities of fresh noodles for home cooks too busy to make their own.

Chic Ciao restaurant (right) is a far cry from the red-checkered-tablecloth Italian restaurant most Americans grew up with. A sparkling all-white decor with rubber-covered floors bespeaks modern industrial Milan.

On the shores of Lake Como in northern Italy, Luciano Parolari (above) of the Villa d'Este Hotel prepared a sumptuous al fresco feast in the famous gardens of the hotel. Several of his recipes are shared in this volume.

In New York's Little Italy, the Feast of San Gennaro (left) provides a glittering spectacle of lights, with Italian foods cooked on the streets.

In Italian markets both in Italy and in Italian-American communities, freshness is always the prime commodity, be it fish or fruits (right).

So that *Adventures in Italian Cooking* would reflect the best of both countries, we traveled extensively in Italy and the United States. In Italy we were able to research traditional cooking methods, and to explore markets that offered a seemingly endless variety of ingredients. As we happily ate our way through Italy, it became apparent that it is hard, if not impossible, to find a bad meal anywhere in the country. Why? Because of the respect most Italians hold for the finest, freshest ingredients, prepared with simple, straightforward methods.

Back in the United States, we discovered Italian-American communities such as those in New York's Little Italy, San Francisco's North Beach, St. Louis, New Orleans, and South Philadelphia. In these cities-within-cities we found shops owned and run by Italians, catering to Italian tastes, and selling Italian products. If you are fortunate enough to live in a city with a substantial Italian-American population, you have probably already experienced the delights of *prosciutto, amaretti,* and the delicacy known as *gelato*—Italian ice cream, perhaps the crowning glory of that nation's food contributions.

As further background for this book, we spent many hours observing and working alongside first, second, and third generation Italian cooks, who invited us into their kitchens and were willing to share some of their treasured family recipes. In addition, we interviewed professional chefs, and visited delicatessens, cheese makers, city markets, bakeries, pasta factories, olive oil makers, wineries, and other producers of American-made Italian foods. we learned that while there is no adequate American substitute for some authentic Italian foods (for instance, the U.S. now forbids importation of many Italian pork products), most American-made Italian products are perfectly good substitutes.

Italian delicatessens are always exciting for their sights, sounds, smells, and tastes. We explored such food emporiums all the way from San Francisco (upper right) *to the via Napoleone in Milan* (lower right). *Although the American counterparts lack many of the Old World ingredients and products, they abound in ready-to-serve or easy-to-prepare treats for busy cooks. Even if you lack nearby Italian marketplaces, you can still enjoy products via mail from our list on page 16.*

Your Italian Kitchen

Not only is Italian cooking changing, but cooking methods also are changing to suit the needs of the modern kitchen. Microwave and convection-air ovens, iceless ice cream makers, electric *espresso* machines, and other modern conveniences are, inevitably, having an effect on traditional methods of preparation.

For centuries, for example, *pesto* sauce was made by hand-grinding fresh basil in a mortar. Today an excellent *pesto* can be made quickly and easily in the blender or food processor. Most Italian cooks still insist that fresh pasta dough be hand-mixed and kneaded, but the food processor is gaining favor in this area too. Once kneaded, the dough can be put through an electric pasta machine to provide fresh noodles as quickly as the cooking water can be boiled.

Kitchen stores in Italy and America feature a wide range of gadgets, including cheese graters, garlic presses, pizza cutters, and ravioli pins. Consequently, this book reflects up-to-date cooking techniques and time-saving methods. In many cases, recipes will provide you with a choice of traditional and contemporary methods of preparation.

Tools such as the traditional copper pan for making polenta *and the* Moka espresso *maker make Italian cooking more authentic and enjoyable, although similar results can be achieved with equipment you probably already have in your kitchen.*

Italian Kitchen Equipment

There is an infinity of utensils and supplies to choose from, but which ones do you really need? In all probability, you could prepare most of the recipes in this book with kitchen equipment you already own. But authentic equipment and ingredients can add to your own enjoyment in preparation and your guests' delight in the food you've prepared. To help you, we have included lists of essentials, nonessentials, authentic, and luxury equipment from which to choose. Don't despair if you find that our "essential" is your "luxury." Remember: One cook's gadget is another cook's favorite tool.

Essentials

Large pot for cooking pasta; must be able to hold 4 to 6 quarts.

Colander, the larger the better, for quick draining of hot pasta.

Long-handled metal ladle for serving sauces and soups.

Heavy wooden mallet or stainless steel pounder for pounding veal scallops and chicken breasts flat.

Garlic press to mash garlic cloves.

Cheese grater for grating Parmesan, *romano*, and other hard cheeses. Choose either the hand-cranked type, which usually comes with two or three different-sized grating cylinders, or the metal grater over a wooden box, which catches the cheese.

Italian espresso maker for making strong Italian coffee. For authentic *espresso*, buy either the Moka or Napoletana-type *espresso* maker.

Milk steamer for steaming milk used in *cappucino* and *caffè latte*. Milk may be heated in a small saucepan for *caffè latte*, but this method will not produce foamy steamed milk for *cappucino*.

Rolling pin for handmade pasta, preferably a perfectly straight wooden cylinder without handles, about 32 inches long.

Pastry wheel to cut dough for stuffed pastas and to slice pizza.

Baking sheets in several sizes for cookies, breads, and pizzas.

Lasagne pan made of heavy metal, with straight sides and square corners for even cooking (other types of pans may burn the *lasagne* around the edges).

Saucepans in various sizes. Heavy enameled cast iron is recommended.

Pans in several sizes for sautéeing and frying. Thick bottoms are required to prevent sticking. Pans with straight sides work best and are the most versatile.

Skillet with slanted sides, or omelet pan, for making *frittata* (an Italian version of an omelet).

Bake-and-serve dishes in several sizes, for stuffed pastas and other oven-to-table recipes.

Pepper mill for freshly ground pepper.

Food mill for a variety of uses.

Additionally, you'll need several different sizes of good, sharp **knives**, a **long-handled cooking fork**, **wooden spoons** in several sizes, a **vegetable peeler**, **wire whisks**, and a **cutting board**.

Nonessential but Invaluable

Food processor to simplify countless food preparations. With all the garlic to be minced, parsley to be chopped, cheese to be grated, and dough to be mixed, you may find this machine to be essential after all.

Deep fryer, electric or nonelectric. Great for frying pastries.

Pasta machine for kneading, thinning, and cutting dough. The hand-cranked version is suggested here; however, if you make pasta by yourself, the electric model will be much easier for you to work with.

Authentic but Nonessential

Bagna cauda dish with compartment for hot coals to keep the upper sauce-basin warm. Substitute: chafing dish.

Mezza-luna, a two-handled knife shaped like a half-moon, to finely mince fresh vegetables and herbs.

Mortar and pestle for crushing pepper and garlic, and for grinding herbs and spices.

Ravioli pin to divide and seal stuffed pasta. Substitute: pastry wheel and knife.

Ravioli pan to shape and cut ravioli. Substitute: pastry wheel and knife.

Ravioli stamp that is pressed over filled dough to cut out individual squares. Substitute: pastry wheel and knife.

Ravioli cutter to give squares fluted edges as they are cut. Substitute: any fluted pastry wheel.

Gnocchi machine to shape potato dumplings. Substitute: fork-and-finger technique, as described on page 50.

Pizza cutter to slice hot pizza. Substitute: any pastry wheel or sharp knife.

Spaghetti cooker with built-in metal drainer. Though not essential, it is highly recommended. Substitute: large pot and colander.

Spaghetti spoon with prongs for lifting strands of boiling pasta. Available in plastic or wood.

Baking stone for cooking pizza and bread with adobe-oven technique. If you make a lot of pizza or bread, this is essential. Substitute: flat baking sheets (*never* a pizza pan with lip that traps grease) *or* several quarry tiles that can be butted together in the oven.

Paddle, wide, flat, and wooden, to move pizza from kitchen counter to baking stone. Substitute: a piece of heavy cardboard.

Cannoli tubes to make pastry shells for frying. If you make *cannoli*, these are essential. Substitute: aluminum tubing cut at hardware store, as directed on page 85.

Cookie irons, *cialde* and *pizzelle*, to bake wafer-thin cookies over direct heat. Substitute: any Scandinavian cookie iron.

Panettone mold for making Milanese sweet bread. Substitute: 1-pound coffee can or folded-down paper bags, as directed on page 71.

Chestnut roaster to roast fresh chestnuts over an open fire. Substitute: any skillet with a long handle, or a wire basket and tongs with which to move it around.

Asparagus cooker to boil lower half of stalk while tips are steamed. Substitute: any pot with high sides, to keep asparagus upright.

Luxury Items

Electric pasta machine to knead, thin, and cut homemade noodles. Substitute: hand-cranked pasta machine, or your hands and a sharp knife.

Copper polenta **pan** with tapered sides and narrow base to confine thickened *polenta* as it boils. Substitute: any saucepan will work, provided you stir.

Terracotta or clay cooker for baking chicken or meats. Always follow manufacturer's care instructions.

Copper zabaglione **pan** that can be used over direct heat to cook wine custard or sauces. Substitute: a double boiler or small saucepan that will fit over another pot of simmering water. A metal ring converter can be used to hold the top pot.

Coffee roaster to roast beans daily to dark, glossy *espresso* strength. Substitute: good Italian or French roast coffee beans.

Espresso and cappucino **makers, electric or nonelectric,** come in many sizes and shapes, and range from moderate to expensive in price. Substitute: Italian coffee makers that work over direct heat, and a milk steamer or saucepan to warm milk.

Italian Ingredients

You'll probably find that many of the staples and seasonings used in Italian cooking are already on your shelves. Listed here are the most commonly used items. Keep on hand those ingredients that you use and enjoy. Always purchase vegetables, fruits, meats, and other perishable ingredients according to what is in season or the freshest offered in the market.

Anchovies. Purchase flat-boned filets packed in olive oil.

Butter. Frequently used in recipes originating from northern Italy. Sweet butter is preferable to salted, and several sticks can be kept in the freezer.

Capers. Choose the tiny imported *nonpareil* type, pickled in vinegar. If the flavor proves too strong, rinse in warm water before adding to dish.

Cheese. For cooking and grating, Parmesan is the most frequently used Italian cheese. Authentic handmade Parmigiana-Reggiano is produced only in a small section of northern Italy, and under very strict government regulations. It is moist and sweet when cut, very expensive, and may not be available in your area. Try a

mixture of 3 parts domestic Parmesan to 1 part *romano*. Try not to use grated cheese sold in containers on supermarket shelves. See page 79 for information on storing and grating cheese.

Cookies. Keep Italian almond macaroons (*amaretti*) on hand to eat with coffee at meal's end, or to crumble into desserts or over ice cream. They keep indefinitely in tin boxes. Italian markets offer many other long-keeping imported cookies.

Coffee. Double-roasted *espresso* can be purchased as whole beans or already ground. Buy only one week's supply at a time, and store tightly covered in a jar or can in the refrigerator.

Flour. Recipes in this book use all-purpose, unsifted flour unless otherwise specified.

Garlic. Purchase fresh garlic heads that are full and large. Always peel garlic cloves before using. When they are cooked slowly, their flavor is sweet and delicate.

Herbs, spices, and condiments. Grow your own fresh herbs or purchase in markets during growing season. Dry leaves by hanging upside down in a warm, dry place; or purchase dried leaves in small quantities. Powdered or already-ground herbs and spices are not as flavorful as freshly ground, but often they are the only

Italian markets, gourmet shops, even supermarkets offer a vast array of Italian ingredients to keep on hand.

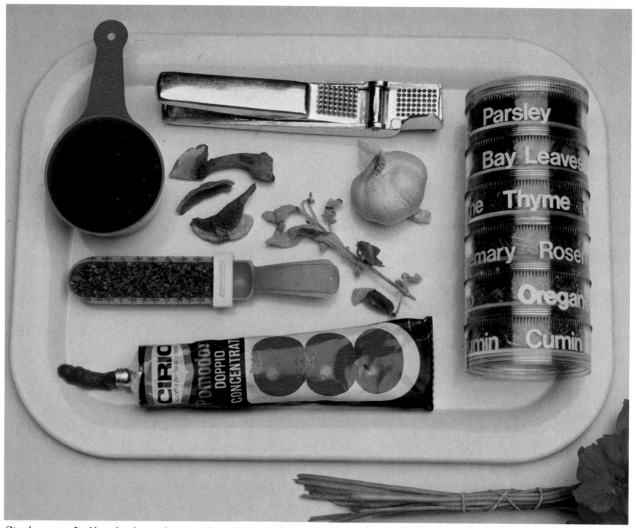

Stock up on Italian herbs, spices, and condiments for your adventure in Italian cooking.

choice. If herbs have been on your shelf for awhile, smell for fragrance and discard if old. The Italian kitchen includes the following herbs, spices, and condiments:

Anise. Sometimes called fennel, it has the unmistakable flavor of licorice. The tiny seeds are used extensively in baking and in making *anisette* liqueur.

Basil. Used to season tomato dishes. Fresh leaves create *pesto* sauce.

Bay leaves. Imported Italian or Greek leaves are more flavorful, but California bay laurel from the supermarket shelves will do. Used to season roast meat and fowl, stews, soups, and stocks.

Marjoram. Northern Italians use this herb to flavor soups and some meats. Similar in flavor to oregano, but much milder.

Oregano. A southern Italian seasoning for tomatoes, fish, salads, and vegetables.

Parsley. Used in countless dishes. Flat-leafed Italian variety has more flavor than the more common curly type.

Pepper. Freshly ground pepper is preferable to pepper sold already ground. Most recipes in this book use black pepper. White pepper is used only in a few, specified recipes, and may be difficult to find in peppercorn form.

Pine nuts (*pignoli*). These small, mild, sweet nuts have a slightly oily flavor. Used in sauces, sweet and sour dishes, cookies, and breads.

Rosemary. Used to flavor roasted fowl or meats, as well as breads and other dishes. Pick leaves off stems and crumble before using.

Saffron. A spice made from the dried stigmas of the crocus plant, with a mild, exotic flavor and a brilliant yellow-orange color. Most famous for its use in *Risotto Milanese*. Use sparingly; this spice is very expensive.

Sage. Flavoring for fowl and meats, especially veal, as well as flat bread and other dishes.

Salt. Like any good cuisine, Italian cooking uses salt in moderation. Since many ingredients are naturally salty (grated cheese, anchovies, capers, pork products), always taste before adding any salt.

Sesame Seeds. Perhaps the oldest condiment known to humanity. Grown for its edible oil and tiny seeds, which are used in baking and sprinkled over breads, rolls, and cookies.

Thyme. An herb plant also used as a garden ornamental. The leaves have a distinct aromatic fragrance and a mild, spicy flavor. Used to flavor fish, sausages, and fresh tomatoes.

Marsala. A sweet wine used to make *zabaglione* and to flavor sauces and other dishes. Sometimes available in almond flavor. Substitute: sweet port wine.

Olive oil. Look for olive oil that has a distinctive flavor reminiscent of the olive fruit, and a pale green color (taste and color vary like wine, according to origin and preparation). Price is not a determining factor for good olive oil; taste is the only reliable test. Good oil may come from Sicily, France, Greece, Spain, or California. Olive oil is *never* refrigerated. Decant the opened olive oil into small uncorked bottles and store in a cool, dustfree cupboard. If you do not use opened oil frequently, taste to check whether it has turned rancid before using.

Olive oils, like wine, are available in a vast range of quality, taste, and color. You may decant large, more economical cans into small glass bottles or the traditional olive oil can for controlled drizzling. In any case, never refrigerate olive oil.

Some recipes in this book call for oil or vegetable oil. In this case, do *not* use olive oil. The flavor will be undesirable. Never use anything on an Italian salad other than good-quality olive oil, and never substitute another oil in a recipe calling for olive oil.

Olives. Keep both black ripe and green olives on hand for cooking and eating as appetizers.

Pancetta. Unsmoked, rolled Italian-style bacon, cured in salt and spices. *Pancetta* from Italy, like other pork products, is not allowed in the U.S.; but good American-made *pancetta* is often available. Purchase from Italian markets or ask your butcher to secure for you. Have it sliced to order: thinly for eating, like other coldcuts, or in a thick slab to use for cooking. Tightly wrapped in plastic, it can be stored for up to three weeks in the refrigerator, or longer in the freezer.

Pasta. For authentic Italian taste and consistency, purchase only imported dried pasta products made from durum wheat or *semolina*. When you find a good one, stock up on various sizes and shapes. It keeps indefinitely. Most American-made dried pasta is made from another kind of flour and is very difficult to cook to the proper *al dente* (firm "to the tooth") stage. It always gets soft and mushy, undesirable qualities in Italian pasta dishes.

Polenta. Italian cornmeal comes finely or coarsely ground. For making *polenta*, the coarsely ground type (either yellow or white) is more interesting texturally. Substitute: stoneground American cornmeal.

Rice. Italian rice, a variety called *arborio*, is shorter and thicker than American rice, but is often hard to find in the United States. Short-grained pearl rice is a good substitute when making *risotto*.

Semolina. The hard, coarse part of the durum wheat grain is used to make Roman-style *gnocchi*, crisp pizza dough, and homemade pasta.

Tomatoes. Fresh, vine-ripened Italian plum tomatoes are the best, especially for sauces. If you don't have a garden, or can't find them at the market, canned Italian-style plum tomatoes are a good substitute. Fresh, round tomatoes can be used, but these are not as flavorful and add more liquid to the sauce.

Tomato paste. Most recipes call for a small amount of tomato paste, leaving the cook with the problem of what to do with the rest of the can. A good, economical solution is to freeze the excess. Put leftover tomato paste by the tablespoonful on a nonstick baking sheet and flash-freeze in the freezer. Then wrap frozen mounds of tomato paste and store in the freezer for use in other recipes. Thick paste is also now available in tubes, like toothpaste, and proves to be very economical.

Tomato sauce. Homemade sauce is far more flavorful than the catsup-like canned type. Using our recipe on page 36, it can be made quickly anytime with canned tomatoes, or prepared in quantity with fresh tomatoes and kept frozen in small containers for later use.

Truffles (*tartufi*). A very expensive delicacy that few Americans have ever tasted. Canned white truffles are available in specialty stores, gourmet sections, and Italian delicatessens.

Tuna. High-quality, costly Italian tuna is packed in olive oil. Substitute: any canned tuna packed in olive oil *or* flake white tuna packed in water, drained, covered with olive oil, and marinated several hours.

Wild mushrooms. Pungent dried mushrooms used to season sauces and other dishes may be bought in Italian markets and stored indefinitely in tightly closed containers. Soak in water to plump before using, and add the mushroom-flavored water to stocks.

Wine. Keep both red and white wine on hand for cooking (see page 26 for more information about Italian wines). Wine used in cooking should be of good, drinkable quality. Never use "cooking wines" to which salt has been added.

Mail Order Sources

At the time of publication, the following businesses offered their merchandise by mail. Write for catalogues to see what is available.

*The Professional Kitchen
18 Cooper Square
New York, NY 10003
(Italian kitchen
equipment.)*

*Williams-Sonoma
P.O. Box 3792
San Francisco, CA
94119
(Italian kitchen
equipment.)*

*Garden Way Country
Kitchen
Charlotte, VT 05445
(Italian kitchen
equipment.)*

*Conte di Savoia
555 W. Roosevelt Road
Chicago, IL 60607
(Italian kitchen
equipment and
ingredients.)*

*Manganaro's Foods
488 Ninth Avenue
New York, NY 10018
(Italian kitchen
equipment and
ingredients.)*

*Todaro Brothers
555 Second Avenue
New York, NY 10016
(Italian ingredients.)*

*D. G. Molinari and Sons
1401 Yosemite Avenue
San Francisco, CA 94124
(Italian ingredients.)*

*G. B. Ratto and Co.,
International Grocers
821 Washington Street
Oakland, CA 94607
(Italian ingredients.)*

The old-fashioned Italian market offers ingredients such as polenta *in bulk.*

ITALIAN COOKING HINTS

Learn to use your kitchen to simplify Italian-style cookery. For example, your regular baking area can easily convert to a pasta-making center. You'll need a smooth surface about 24 inches square for mixing, kneading, rolling, and cutting pasta dough. A thick plastic or formica countertop will do. Wood is acceptable, although it is porous and absorbs odors.

Within easy reach you'll need sharp knives, a rolling pin, and a container of flour. The same work surface then makes way for your hand-cranked or electric pasta machine to complete the kneading and do the cutting quickly. Clean towels spread on the kitchen table or another unused counter make a good place to lay the noodles out to dry. Or you can install a metal or wooden dowel rod beneath the kitchen windows or underneath an upper cabinet where you can hang noodle strands up to dry completely out of your way.

Keep a few things in your refrigerator or freezer for last-minute Italian cooking inspirations. Even if you haven't had time to shop, a package or two of homemade or locally made fresh **fettuccine** and a container of summer-fresh **pesto** sauce (page 36), or a cup of long-simmered meat sauce can produce a great Italian dinner. Keep a container of Herb-Seasoned Breadcrumbs (page 71) handy in your refrigerator, as most good Italian cooks do. They can quickly turn a simple meat or vegetable dish into gourmet fare.

Other good items to keep on hand in the freezer include homemade chicken or meat stock (page 27); a bag of bones and trimmings for future stocks; homemade tomato sauce (page 36); chopped spinach or artichokes to throw into a quick omelet; leftover grated cheese to sprinkle into soups or sauces; and tiny peas.

Microwave ovens make thawing frozen items a breeze. They can also be adapted to a full range of Italian cooking.

Italian Recipes:

Antipasto to Zabaglione

The pace and style of Italian dining are quite different from what we are used to in the United States. Instead of working hard all day and rushing home to a big dinner, the major meal in Italy comes at midday. Until quite recently, most people stopped work and went home to enjoy a leisurely meal. With increasing urbanization, however, many contemporary Italians tend to stay downtown and eat their big noontime meal in restaurants.

Instead of concentrating on one main course with side dishes, as we do, the Italian meal consists of many courses, each served individually. The evening meal may be a scaled-down version of the noon meal, or just a bowl of soup, some cheese and bread, or a late-night snack of pizza, pasta, or a toasted sandwich.

Breakfast is simple, consisting of plenty of strong *espresso* combined with hot milk (*caffè latte*), and fresh bread spread with butter and jam. Coffee is consumed throughout the day,

The large main meal begins with appetizers (*antipasti*) to stimulate the appetite for the first course (*primo*). This may be either soup, pasta, rice (*risotto*), dumplings (*gnocchi*), or cornmeal (*polenta*). The first course is enjoyed for its own sake, and is rarely served alongside the second course, as is customary in America. Like *antipasti*, the first course is always served in small portions to leave room for the rest of the meal.

Teamed for great beginnings are apertivi *to mix with sparkling soda water and* antipasti *of chilled seasonal fruits and sliced* proscuitto.

The second course (*secondo*) is usually meat, poultry, or fish that has been roasted, stewed, baked, grilled, sautéed, or fried. A vegetable side dish (*contorno*) may accompany the course.

Next comes a crisp palate-cleansing salad. This may be a simple salad of tossed fresh greens, or vegetables served either raw or slightly cooked and lightly dressed.

Cheese is enjoyed as its own course, or in combination with fruit. A piece of cheese with crusty bread may be followed by fruit prepared as a light dessert.

Italy has created some wonderful sweets, but they're rarely served at the end of the meal. They're usually eaten in pastry shops, cafes, or at home as afternoon treats with coffee or a glass of wine. The Italian meal ends with *caffè espresso*. Liqueur may follow the coffee or accompany it, and wine and mineral water are enjoyed throughout the meal.

Appetizers (Antipasti)

The word *antipasto* is derived from *anti* (before) and *pasto* (meal). Thus the *antipasto* is designed to stimulate one's appetite for the rest of the meal. But Italian appetizers, with their attractive colors, shapes, textures, and wonderful aromas, capture all the senses.

The composition of the *antipasto* follows no set rules, but is a product of local, regional, and seasonal ingredients. In restaurants, *antipasti* may be many and varied; indeed, this course can be a meal in itself. But at the family table, matters are more restrained. Here the choice of *antipasti* is governed by one principle: Be moderate, or you won't enjoy your meal. The course you serve at home, therefore, is more likely to consist of one or two simple foods, usually with an emphasis on freshness. Like the rest of the meal, an *antipasto* should reflect the best of the season's bounty—cool melon, fresh seafood, or vegetables just picked from the garden.

But there is no need to feel hampered by a lack of fresh ingredients. *Antipasti* offer the cook a chance to be really creative. When fresh ingredients are unavailable, or just to add variety, good Italian cooks never hestitate to supplement with jars and cans of tasty prepared foods such as marinated vegetables (*giardiniera*) or roasted marinated peppers (*peperoni*). Similarly, the delicatessen can provide you with Italian olives or a few slices of *prosciutto*. Many dishes that might ordinarily be served later on the menu or even as leftovers turn up on the Italian table as *antipasti*. *Antipasti* may be served singly or in combination; on individual plates or from one big platter; at the dinner table as well as in the living room; or on the patio with an *aperitivo*.

Assorted Appetizers (Antipasti Assorti)

In larger U.S. and Canadian cities, a survey of local gourmet market shelves and Italian delicatessen cases can turn up many prepared items that make tasty, quick appetizers. Any of the following can be used in *antipasti assorti*, or served alone.

Anchovies. Serve filets drizzled with olive oil and garnished with strips of red pepper, capers, and lemon wedges *or* buy anchovies that are already wrapped around capers.

Artichoke hearts in olive oil. Serve these garnished with strips of roasted peppers, by themselves, or tossed in green salads.

Caponata. The canned version of eggplant relish is good, but doesn't come close to our recipe (page 22).

Consider how easy it is to put together a dazzling tray of Antipasti Assorti from the wide range of available canned appetizers. Use such commercially prepared, domestic or imported products alone or to supplement your own appetizers made from the accompanying recipes.

Cheese. Combine Italian cheeses such as *fontina* or *provolone* with sliced coldcuts or raw vegetables.

Coldcuts. Italian coldcuts include *coppa, prosciutto, mortadella,* and *salami*. Sample coldcuts at an Italian deli to find your favorites.

Fava beans. Drain canned beans, rinse well, and combine with 3 parts olive oil to 1 part wine vinegar, chopped green onion, and salt and freshly ground black pepper to taste. Allow to marinate several hours before serving.

Fish paté. Tubes of Italian smoked trout, sturgeon, and other fish are available in Italian grocery stores. Squeeze a bit on crackers or small pieces of toast.

Giardiniera. These mixed pickled vegetables may be offered in a bowl, or as a garnish for other ingredients.

Italian tuna or sardines in olive oil. Delicious with lemon juice or a bit of homemade mayonnaise and a sprinkling of capers.

Jellied cured beef slices. Good with mustard or horseradish sauce; available at Italian delicatessens.

Marinated mushrooms. Available canned or from the deli case.

Olives. Both the dried black and marinated green olives are best purchased at an Italian delicatessen.

Peperoncini. Peppers preserved in vinegar are indispensable to the *antipasto* platter.

Prosciutto. Salty, yet sweet cured ham can be found in most Italian delicatessens. Varies in flavor and texture, depending on origin. Usually served very thinly sliced; wonderful wrapped around bread sticks or fruits.

Rice salad. Available in jars, or easily made from our recipe (page 23).

Roasted marinated peppers. Your choice of red, yellow, or green. The taste is quite different from fresh sweet peppers. Purchase in jars or roast your own according to our directions (page 76).

Tuna and vegetables in tomato sauce. Usually sold in jars labeled "*antipasto*." Serve on individual salad plates or as part of the *antipasto* platter.

CREATING YOUR OWN ANTIPASTI

Try these combinations accompanied by a loaf of crusty Italian or French bread, or the long, crisp, slender breadsticks called **grissini**.

Alternate slices of fresh sweet red, yellow, and green peppers with slices of **fontina** cheese.

Arrange fresh clams or oysters on the halfshell on a bed of crushed ice. Garnish with lemon slices and accompany with your favorite seafood cocktail sauce or serve your favorite seafood cocktail.

Boil fava beans in salted water until tender, shell, and sprinkle with freshly grated **pecorino** or **romano** cheese.

Stuff a small, peeled tomato with marinated **calamari** (squid), Italian tuna, or any fish salad.

Stuff colossal-sized pitted black olives with chopped anchovies and capers. Marinate in olive oil for several hours before serving.

Slice garden-ripe tomatoes and sprinkle with minced fresh basil. Drizzle with good olive oil and a bit of freshly squeezed lemon juice.

Roll a slice of **mortadella** around a strip of roasted pepper. Top with a small gherkin or a ripe olive.

Serve small portions of any of the salads listed on pages 75 to 78.

Cut a **frittata** (page 64) into small wedges. Serve warm or at room temperature.

Blend tiny shrimp with olive oil and lemon juice, and sprinkle with parsley.

Halve hard-cooked eggs, blend yolks with anchovy paste, and restuff whites.

Combine **garbanzo** beans or red kidney beans with olive oil, wine vinegar, chopped green onions, and minced parsley.

Coldcuts with Fresh Fruits

Perhaps the most refreshing beginning to a warm-weather meal is the classic combination of thinly sliced **prosciutto** and sweet cantaloupe.

Prosciutto and freshly peeled figs provide another simple, delectable **antipasto**.

For variation, combine any good coldcuts—Italian or any of your favorites—with sliced papaya, kiwi fruit, light or dark figs, strawberries, pears, or melons.

Italian Mayonnaise (Maionese)

Homemade **maionese** tastes so superior to the commercial blends that you'll want to use it in all recipes calling for mayonnaise, and as a sauce or dip for a variety of **antipasti**.

Italian mayonnaise differs from other versions in two ways: no mustard is added, and lemon juice is preferred to vinegar. The time-honored method of mayonnaise-making is to beat the oil in with a spoon, drop by drop. But in the modern Italian kitchen, **maionese** can be made quickly and easily in the food processor or blender. Always begin with all ingredients at room temperature

2 egg yolks
2 tablespoons freshly squeezed lemon juice
1 teaspoon salt
1 to 1½ cups olive oil or vegetable oil (for a more delicate flavor)

1. Place egg yolks in a blender or food processor bowl. Add lemon juice and salt; blend for a few seconds.

2. With motor running, add oil gradually in a very slow, steady trickle. Blend until **maionese** is thick and creamy. Add more salt and lemon juice to taste, if desired.

Makes about 1 cup

Note. Store covered in the refrigerator.

For elegant dining, Carpaccio is a tasty appetizer easily prepared by slicing frozen raw steak. A mustard sauce is spread over the beef at the table.

Chilled Raw Beef with Mustard Sauce (Carpaccio)

Tender, raw beef, sliced paper thin and enlivened with mustard sauce, is a fine beginning to the Italian meal.

Lean, boneless top round or sirloin, ¼ pound per person
Mustard Sauce (recipe follows)
Capers
Watercress or **parsley, and radish** or **cherry tomato for garnish**

1. Freeze meat until just firm enough to slice easily with a large, very sharp knife. At serving time, slice very thinly and arrange overlapping pieces on a plate. The beef will thaw almost as soon as it hits the plate.

Mustard Sauce

1 cup homemade
  Maionese or prepared mayonnaise
2 teaspoons Dijon mustard
2 teaspoons freshly squeezed lemon juice

Top with a dollop of Mustard Sauce, sprinkle with capers, and garnish.

Note. If you need a large quantity of beef for entertaining—and you're on good terms with your butcher—have the beef frozen, sliced, and wrapped in plastic wrap at the market. Store chilled until serving time.

Combine maionese, mustard, and lemon juice with a fork until well blended.

Cold Eggplant Appetizer (Caponata)

Caponata, a very old favorite in Sicily, is a tangy spread made with eggplant that can also serve as a salad or relish. Consider making it in quantity when the garden is at its peak, and preserving it in jars for year-round enjoyment.

2 medium eggplants
¾ cup olive oil
2 onions, sliced
¼ cup canned tomato sauce or 1 fresh tomato, peeled, chopped, and sautéed in olive oil until soft
2 celery stalks, diced
¼ cup capers, well drained
6 Italian-style green olives, pitted and cut into quarters
1 tablespoon pine nuts
2 tablespoons red or white wine vinegar
2 tablespoons sugar
½ teaspoon salt
¼ teaspoon freshly ground black pepper

1. Peel and dice eggplant and sauté in ½ cup of the olive oil until golden brown. Remove eggplant from skillet and reserve. Add remaining oil and onions and cook until onions are soft and golden. Add tomato sauce and celery. Cook until celery is tender, stirring occasionally. If necessary, add a little hot water to prevent sticking. Add capers, olives, pine nuts, and reserved eggplant.

2. Heat vinegar and dissolve sugar in it; add salt and pepper. Pour liquid over eggplant mixture. Simmer, covered, over very low heat for 20 minutes, stirring frequently. Chill thoroughly before serving.

Store in a tightly covered jar in the refrigerator for up to two weeks.

Makes 6 servings.

Note. To preserve, pour hot mixture into sterilized half-pint jars. Seal and process in boiling water bath for 25 minutes.

Menu suggestions. This dish teams up well with other appetizers. It may also be served as a relish with grilled meats. Serve small portions on a lettuce leaf as a salad course.

22

Hot Dip for Raw Vegetables (Bagna Cauda)

Abundant yields of garden-fresh vegetables inspired the cooks of Piedmont to create this spectacular, easily prepared, and heartwarming dish. It is one of the most renowned specialties of that region.

Literally, **Bagna cauda** means "hot bath," and it is just that—a hot anchovy dip for raw vegetables. As with fondue, the pleasure in eating lies in sharing and dipping into the communal pot.

Old World tradition calls for cooking **Bagna cauda** in an earthenware pot at the fireside, but today it is quite appropriately served in a chafing dish, fondue pot, or an earthenware pot placed over a candle warmer or anything that provides just enough heat to keep the sauce hot without cooking it further.

The time-honored way to eat **Bagna cauda** is to dip vegetables with one hand, while holding a piece of bread with the other to catch drips. Of course, you won't be able to resist dipping the bread into the sauce from time to time to scoop up more of the flavorful, aromatic sauce.

¼ **cup olive oil**
¾ **cup butter**
4 **cloves garlic, finely minced**
2 **ounces** or **one small can flat anchovy filets, drained and mashed Salt, if desired**

1. In an earthenware pot, heat oil and butter until butter is melted and begins to foam. Sauté garlic briefly (do not allow to color). Add anchovies and stir over very low heat until sauce is smooth. Taste and add salt, if necessary.

2. Place pot over candle warmer and serve with generous amounts of raw vegetables and crusty Italian or French bread.

Variations. Add one of the following to the hot dip after the anchovies have been blended in: 1 canned white truffle, finely minced **or** 2 tablespoons finely chopped toasted walnuts.

Makes 8 to 10 servings

Vegetables for dipping. Your presentation will be more dramatic if you leave most vegetables in whole form, making a few necessary cuts in the kitchen so they can easily be broken into bite-sized pieces at the table.

For immediate serving, prepare vegetables by rinsing in cold water and patting as dry as possible. Arrange on a tray or in a basket.

Vegetables can also be prepared several hours ahead. Prepare as above and wrap in plastic or foil and keep chilled until serving time.

The original Piedmont version of **Bagna cauda** calls for small, sweet cardoons. We either have to grow our own, or cut only the hearts from large, tough ones sometimes available in Italian vegetable markets. Sweet anise or fennel is an excellent substitute, as is celery. Italian-American cooks freely add whatever is available from the garden or greengrocer. Some prefer to serve steamed and chilled vegetables such as broccoli and carrots in addition to the above, as long as they are not overcooked. They must be crisp to the bite.

Additional suggestions. Use cooked artichoke hearts, asparagus, cauliflower, cherry tomatoes, Jerusalem artichokes, mushrooms, sweet peppers, radishes, or zucchini.

Menu suggestions. The **Bagna cauda** pot should be placed in the middle of the table so guests can sit all around it. Provide plenty of napkins. Follow it with roast meat, broiled fowl, or any type of simply prepared meat. It is quite rich and extremely filling.

Rice Salad (Insalata di Riso)

Called a salad, but never served as the salad course, this cold seasoned rice may be included as part of the **antipasto**, or it can be expanded into a first course, picnic fare, or summer meal by adding diced cooked chicken, flaked tuna, boiled shrimp, or other seafood. Increase amount of dressing when you add fish or fowl.

1 **cup raw Italian** arborio or **short-grained pearl rice**
½ **cup thinly sliced pitted black olives**
½ **red, yellow, or green sweet pepper, cored, seeded, and diced** or **roasted pepper, chopped**
2 **tablespoons tiny capers**
½ **cup finely diced** fontina **cheese (or substitute any Swiss)**
¼ **cup chopped parsley**
¼ **cup sliced green onions**
⅓ **cup olive oil**
1 **tablespoon wine vinegar**
1 **teaspoon Dijon mustard Salt and freshly ground black pepper to taste**

1. Cook rice according to package directions, until tender but still firm to the bite.

2. Place well-drained rice in bowl and add olives, peppers, capers, cheese, parsley, and onions.

3. Combine oil, vinegar, mustard, salt, and pepper in small bowl. Blend well with fork and pour over salad. Toss thoroughly and serve slightly chilled.

Serves 4 to 6.

Hollowed-out pepper shells create colorful containers for Rice Salad. Expand the dish into a summer meal by adding cold cooked meats or fish.

Melted Cheese Sauce (Fonduta)

A distant relative of cheese fondue, this dish originated in Piedmont and is based on two ingredients native to that region: white truffles and smooth-melting **fontina** cheese. Unlike its Swiss and French counterparts, however, **Fonduta** contains no alcohol and is not served in a chafing dish. Rather, it is served in a bowl for dipping, or poured directly over sliced or toasted bread, rice, or **polenta**.

Fonduta can put in an appearance as an **antipasto, primo** or **secondo**, or as a great late-night snack or fireside supper.

Since fresh white truffles are almost impossible to get and prohibitively expensive when they are available, you will probably resort to canned white truffles, which are still on the expensive side. **Fonduta** is delicious even without the truffle addition.

Try to find real Italian **fontina** for this recipe. If you can't, go with another smoothly melting cheese such as Gruyere from Switzerland or the red-rind Danish version of **fontina**. Although the outcome will not be as good, it's still a tasty dish.

1½ teaspoons cornstarch
1 cup light cream
1½ pounds Italian fontina cheese, cut into small pieces
Salt and freshly ground white pepper
4 egg yolks
1 or 2 fresh or canned small white truffles, sliced as thinly as possible (optional)
Crusty Italian or French bread, sliced fresh or toasted, cut into wedges or triangles

1. Dissolve cornstarch in ¾ cup of the light cream in a heavy saucepan with cheese, and salt and pepper to taste. Stir constantly over low heat until cheese melts, about 5 minutes. At this stage it may be stringy.

2. Blend egg yolks and the remaining ¼ cup milk. Add about ¼ cup of the melted cheese to the egg yolk mixture, beating well to blend. Slowly return the egg and cheese mixture to the pot, beating constantly. Cook the mixture over low heat until creamy smooth, then pour into a preheated bowl and top with sliced truffles, if available. Surround with bread or toast.

Makes 6 servings.

Menu Suggestions. Serve in small ramekins for individual appetizers, followed by pasta that does not use cheese in its preparation. Instead, try something light like Spaghetti with Peas and **Prosciutto** (page 67), and a simple second course.

As a second course, **Fonduta** may be preceded by Stuffed Zucchini (page 68) or Stuffed Artichoke (page 65) or pasta, as recommended above. You'll want some sort of crunchy salad to follow.

For an elegant late-night supper serve only the truffle-topped **Fonduta**, a tossed green salad, and accompany with a bottle of sparkling dessert wine.

Broiled Marinated Shrimp (Gamberetti all' Olio e Limone)

1 pound shrimp, shelled and deveined (if large, cut in half)
½ cup olive oil
½ cup lemon juice
3 cloves garlic, crushed
Salt and freshly ground black pepper to taste
¼ cup Herb-Seasoned Breadcrumbs (page 71)
Butter
Lemon slices and chopped parsley for garnish

1. Combine all ingredients except breadcrumbs and butter. Refrigerate several hours or overnight. Drain marinade.

2. Distribute evenly among four scallop shells or individual baking dishes. Sprinkle with breadcrumbs and dot with butter.

3. Place under broiler for about 5 minutes or until bubbly. Don't overcook.

4. Garnish with lemon slices and parsley.

Makes 4 servings.

Squid marinade (Calamari Marinati)

Adventurous cooks and diners will find this one of the tastiest beginnings to an Italian meal. Squid is usually available at larger fish markets, or you can probably find it frozen at a large supermarket. Cleaning is easy once you get the hang of it.

2 pounds cleaned squid, whole
4 quarts boiling salted water
1 cup chopped onion
¾ cup sliced celery or bulbous fennel
½ cup chopped parsley
¼ cup chopped fresh basil or 1 teaspoon dried basil
1 tablespoon minced fresh oregano or 1 teaspoon dried oregano
3 cloves garlic, finely minced
¾ cup olive oil
¼ cup wine vinegar
Juice of 1 lemon
Salt and freshly ground black pepper to taste

How to clean squid. (See photos on page 63). If you are not able to purchase cleaned squid, you will have to clean them yourself. Hold squid under cold running water and pull speckled membrane from sac. Holding the sac in one hand, gently pull off the tentacles. Contents of sac should come out attached to tentacles.

To separate tentacles from sac, slice horizontally just above the eyes. Pull out horny beaked mouth and discard. Wash tentacles in cold water, pat dry, and put aside.

Pull out any remaining contents from inside sac and discard. Rinse sac and pat dry. If squid are to be sliced, slice sac horizontally to make ¼- to ½-inch-wide rings. Leave tentacles whole.

1. Drop cleaned squid into boiling water in a large kettle. Return to boil and cook until tender, about 20 minutes. Drain and cool. Cut sac into rings, tentacles into small clusters, and place in a large bowl.

2. Add remaining ingredients and toss thoroughly. Cover tightly and refrigerate at least 24 hours, stirring from time to time. Drain marinade before serving.

Makes 6 to 8 servings.

Menu suggestions. A delicious appetizer for an all-fish dinner, or preceding simple pasta preparations.

Fried Cheese (Formaggio Fritto)

For this hot appetizer, slices of cheese are quickly fried inside a coating of seasoned breadcrumbs.

¾ cup fine dry breadcrumbs
⅛ teaspoon dried oregano, crushed
¼ teaspoon salt
2 cloves garlic, finely minced
1 egg, beaten
2 tablespoons milk
Vegetable oil
6 ounces firm cheese (cheddar, mozzarella, jack), cut into ½-inch-thick slices
¾ cup flour

1. Mix breadcrumbs, oregano, salt, and garlic in a small bowl. In another bowl combine egg and milk.

2. Heat a 2-inch layer of oil in a deep heavy skillet over medium-high heat until hot, but not smoking.

3. While oil is heating, quickly dip the individual cheese slices first into flour, next into whipped egg mixture, and then coat generously with seasoned breadcrumbs. Let coated cheese sit uncovered in a single layer for 10 to 15 minutes to dry. If necessary, repeat process so that crumbs completely cover cheese.

4. Slide coated slices into hot oil. Fry until golden brown, turning once. Total frying time will be about 2 minutes. Drain for just a moment on paper towels. Serve piping hot.

Makes 6 servings.

Drinks (Bibite)

Every well-set Italian table has both mineral water (*aqua minerale*) and wine (*vino*). Each may be enjoyed separately, or they may be poured together. Especially on hot days, Italians often splash a bit of mineral water into the wine, or vice-versa, to create a cool drink.

Although the vast majority of Italians drink wine with meals, you may prefer another beverage. Consider alternatives that are still Italian in spirit: fresh juices (*succo di frutta*), lemonade (*limonata*), orange soda (*aranciata*), and soft drinks made from Italian soda syrups and sparkling water.

Mineral Water (Aqua Minerale)

Aqua minerale may be either sparkling (*gassata*) or plain (*naturale*). The bubbly version may be natural from the spring, or with added carbon dioxide. Your choice of label will depend on local availability; there are almost as many producers and labels of *aqua minerale* as there are Italian wine makers. You can, of course, serve mineral waters or wines from California, France, or elsewhere with Italian foods.

Always serve mineral water well chilled, with or without ice. You may add a twist or slice of lemon or lime to freshen the taste and add some color.

Sparkling or plain mineral waters from Italy (above) *compliment any meal. Enjoy noncaloric waters alone or in combination with wine, varying proportions according to your taste. Try various brands to find those you like. Italian soda syrups* (right) *mixed with bubbly mineral water or club soda create a not-too-sweet treat to delight all ages.*

Italian Sodas (Soda)

Imported bottled syrups come in an array of interesting flavors, from the exotic (cassis, grenadine, orgeat) to the familiar (lime, cherry, strawberry). Simply combine 1 part concentrated syrup with 6 parts sparkling mineral water or club soda. You may add more or less syrup according to personal preference. Fill glasses with ice and add a garnish of fresh fruit or a sprig of mint.

To create an Italian ice cream soda, pour the syrups over ice cream (vanilla is compatible with everything) and fill the glass with sparkling water. Similarly, you can make Italian snow cones by pouring syrup over mounds of finely crushed ice.

Before-Dinner Drinks (Aperitivi)

The word *aperitivo* means different things to different people. To many wine buffs there are but three *aperitivi*, none of which are Italian: dry sherry, dry vermouth, and *brut* champagne. But in a more general sense, *aperitivo* denotes any drink taken to stimulate the palate and whet the appetite. In this view, there are no hard-and-fast rules, although sweet, heavy drinks should be avoided. Some popular Italian *aperitivi* are Cinzano, Italian vermouth, Cynar, and Campari.

Wines (Vini)

Italy produces more wine than any other country. Until recently, however, excellent Italian wine tended to stay in Italy. Two things happened to change all that: the rising cost of good French and California wines, and the passage of the *Denominazione di Origine Controllata* (DOC), which officially guarantees and delimits a wine in much the same way as does the French *Appellation d'Origine Controlée*.

When purchasing Italian wines, you may feel confused by the profusion of names and labels (there are over thirty-five DOC wines from the Piedmont region alone). A wine merchant can be a good source of advice, and the following list will tell you what to keep in mind.

Classico. This word can only appear on a label if the wine comes from the best or central part of the general area of production. It is sometimes an indication of a very good wine, but not always.

Consorzio. A *consorzio* is an association of wine producers. A small label affixed to the wine bottle names the *consorzio* responsible for producing the wine. The presence of this label does not assure quality, but you may find that you prefer the wine of one *consorzio* over another.

DOC. If the words *Denominazione di Origine Controllata* are on the label, the consumer can be sure that (1) the wine is from the area named, (2) the vintage year is accurate, and (3) production and aging methods have been carried out properly.

DOS. These wines are not as outstanding as DOC wines.

DOCG. These wines are superior to DOC wines.

Marchio Nazionale. A small red label on the neck bears the letters "INE." This label simply certifies the wine as drinkable. If the bottle also shows the DOC label, this is at least an indication of quality in a bottle of wine.

Riserva, Riserva Speciale, and Superiore. These words on the label indicate that the wine has been aged longer than is considered normal, and should thus be of better quality than the same wines whose labels are not so marked.

Serving Wine. The basics for serving Italian wine are the same as for any other wine. The oldest rule is based on general usage: white before red, dry before sweet, young before old, light before heavy.

Another general rule is to serve white wines with fish and poultry, red wines with meat or heavily spiced dishes, dessert wines with dessert.

It is a good idea to stand a bottle of red wine upright for a few days before serving. This will allow any sediment to settle to the bottom. Old wines that are known to throw much sediment should be disturbed as little as possible. In some cases, decanting may be called for.

The best all-purpose glass for red and white wines is a clear tulip-shaped glass. It should be fairly large, capable of holding at least 6 ounces of liquid, even though it won't be filled to more than ⅓ capacity.

Finding the Italian wines that go best with your meals is simply a matter of taste. Your wine merchant and the information here can help you make some good buys.

TYPES OF ITALIAN WINES

Following is a list of Italian wines, divided into specific types. The list is not complete, and includes only those Italian wines that are usually available.

White wines.
Mellow whites. Frascati, Est! Est! Est!, Frascati Secco, Moscato d'Asti, Pinot Secco, Pinot Bianco, Pinot Grigio.
Dry, medium-bodied whites. Orvieto Secco, Soave, Verdicchio.,

Red wines.
Semi-dry red. Lambrusco.
Dry, light-bodied red. Bardolino.
Dry, medium-bodied reds. Chianti, Dolcetto, Grignolino, Grumello, Merlot, Nebbiolo, Valpolicella
Robust reds. Barbera, Barbaresco, Barolo, Brunello di Montal-cino, Chianti Classico, Gattinara, Ghemme.

Dessert Wines. Asti Spumante, Marsala, Moscato.

Sparkling Wines. Asti Spumante, Spumante Brut.

First Courses (Primi Piatti)

Primo, the first course, may be either soup, pasta, *risotto*, *polenta*, or *gnocchi*. Serve only *one* of these (do not, for example, serve soup followed by pasta).

Soups (Minestre)

Italians love soup. It frequently starts the meal, and quite often is a light evening meal all by itself. A stock or broth made with meat, fowl, fish, or vegetables is called *brodo*. It may be served plain, or contain tiny pasta, rice, bits of meat, or other ingredients. *Brodo* is also the base for making thicker soups, and is used in the preparation of dishes such as *risotto*.

Thick, hearty soups are called *minestrone*. These are composed of a variety of vegetables and meat, and usually include either pasta *or* rice—but never the two in the same soup. In addition to these there are creamed soups, vegetable soups, and many more.

In Italian homes soup is served from soup plates rather than from bowls, and is eaten with a spoon that resembles a serving tablespoon rather than the rounded, medium-sized spoons that Americans seem to favor. A bowl of grated Parmesan cheese is almost always served at the table, to be sprinkled over the soup at the diner's discretion.

Chicken Broth or Stock (Brodo di Pollo)

2 pounds lean soup meat, such as brisket or shank
2 beef marrow bones, cracked
4 quarts water
2 medium onions, sliced
1 large carrot, peeled and cut into chunks
1 celery stalk, with green leaves, cut into pieces
1/2 cup parsley, with stems
2 bay leaves
3 whole cloves
1 tablespoon salt
8 whole peppercorns

1. In a large, deep soup kettle, cover meat and marrow bones with water. Bring to boil over high heat and skim. Add all the remaining ingredients, bring again to boiling point, and skim.

2. Reduce heat to low, cover, and simmer for 3 to 5 hours, skimming as necessary. If necessary, add more hot water to keep original level of the liquid in the kettle.

3. Skim off any fat and strain soup through several layers of cheesecloth or a fine sieve. Taste and adjust for seasoning. Cool and chill in the refrigerator.

4. The next day, remove any fat that has risen to the top. Keep refrigerated, or freeze in smaller containers. Stock will keep in the refrigerator for about 6 days.

Makes 2 quarts.

Hearty Vegetable Soup (Minestrone)

Minestrone roughly translates as "big first course," but actually this hearty soup is more of a main dish. There is no "authentic" recipe for **minestrone**, and procedures vary from province to province and city to city. Italian cooks usually start with beans, vegetables, and stock or water; beyond that, what goes into the pot depends on what's at hand. Feel free to adapt the following recipe.

2 tablespoons olive oil
2 tablespoons butter
1 cup chopped onion
1 cup chopped carrots
1 cup chopped celery
2 cloves garlic, minced
1/4 cup minced parsley
2 cups peeled and diced potatoes
1 cup sliced zucchini
1 small bunch Swiss chard, chopped
3/4 cup dry white beans, soaked and ready to cook
2 cups chopped Italian-style plum tomatoes, fresh or canned
6 cups homemade Beef Stock or regular-strength canned broth
1/2 teaspoon dried basil
1/4 teaspoon dried thyme
1 bay leaf
Salt and freshly ground black pepper to taste
1/2 cup any small dried pasta
1/2 head cabbage, shredded
2 tablespoons Pesto Sauce (page 36) (optional)
1 cup canned garbanzo beans

Freshly grated Parmesan cheese

1. In a large stockpot, combine olive oil and butter. Add onion, carrots, celery, garlic, and parsley. Sauté until onion is transparent. Add potatoes, zucchini, Swiss chard, beans, and tomatoes; sauté 5 minutes more.

2. Stir in broth, basil, thyme, and bay leaf. Season with salt and pepper to taste. Bring to a boil, cover, and reduce heat. Simmer for 2 hours. (Should soup become too thick, add more stock or water.)

3. Turn heat up to medium-high and add pasta and cabbage. Cook for another 30 minutes, stirring frequently to prevent sticking. Ten minutes before serving, add Pesto Sauce, if desired, and garbanzo beans. Correct seasoning. Serve with grated Parmesan cheese.

Makes 8 servings.

Note. Flavor improves the second day. May be refrigerated for several days.

Beef Stock (Brodo di Manzo)

1 chicken weighing 2 to 3 pounds, cut into pieces
Water to cover
1 stalk celery, with green leaves, cut into pieces
1 large carrot, peeled and cut into chunks
1 onion, quartered
1/4 cup fresh parsley
4 whole black peppercorns
2 whole cloves
2 whole allspice
1 bay leaf
Salt (1/2 teaspoon per pound of chicken)

1. Put the back, wings, and legs of the chicken into the bottom of a large, deep soup kettle, and top with rest of the pieces. Add water, just to cover, and remaining ingredients. Bring to boiling point and skim.

2. Reduce heat to low, cover, and simmer 2 to 3 hours, skimming as necessary. Add more hot water to keep original level of the liquid in the kettle.

3. With a slotted spoon remove the chicken from the kettle and reserve for other uses. Strain the soup through several layers of cheesecloth or a fine sieve. Taste and adjust seasoning if necessary. Cool and chill in the refrigerator.

4. The next day, remove any fat that has risen to the top. Keep refrigerated, or freeze in smaller containers. Stock will keep in the refrigerator for up to 6 days.

Makes 2 quarts.

Freshly shelled peas simmered slowly with rice in broth are featured in one of Italy's most unusual soups, Risi e Bisi.

Escarole Soup (Zuppa di Scarola)

A very simple soup that can be prepared and served within an hour.

⅓ cup butter
1 small onion, minced
1 head escarole, well washed and coarsely chopped
Salt and freshly ground black pepper to taste
4 cups homemade Chicken Broth (page 27) or regular-strength canned broth
¼ cup crushed vermicelli
¼ cup freshly grated Parmesan cheese

1. In a large saucepan, melt butter and sauté onion over medium heat until browned. Add escarole and salt and pepper to taste. Sauté briefly, then add broth. Cover and cook over low heat 15 minutes. Add vermicelli and cook an additional 15 minutes.

2. Taste and season. Serve with freshly grated Parmesan cheese.

Makes 4 servings.

Variation. Prepare with fresh spinach or other greens.

Menu suggestions. Serve before spicy dishes or those containing tomatoes.

Tuscan Bean Soup (Fagioli alla Toscana)

The Tuscans have so many bean dishes that they are often called "bean eaters." All of the bean dishes are worth eating, whether made from the fresh or dried variety. This simple but delicious bean soup is found all over Tuscany.

½ pound white beans
2 quarts water
Salt and freshly ground black pepper to taste
¼ cup olive oil
2 cloves garlic, minced
2 tablespoons minced fresh parsley

1. Soak beans in water overnight. Drain and place in a large pot with 2 quarts water. Simmer for 3 hours or until tender. Put half of the beans through a sieve.

2. Combine purée with rest of beans in pot. Season with salt and pepper to taste.

3. Heat olive oil in a small saucepan and gently brown the minced garlic in it. Add the fresh parsley, stir all together, and pour into soup. Adjust seasoning if necessary.

Serves 6 to 8.

Rice and Peas (Risi e Bisi)

Italian cooks disagree as to whether this Venetian specialty should be classed as a soup or vegetable. It should remain a bit soupy and be served in a bowl, to be eaten with a spoon. It makes a perfect first course.

¼ cup butter
3 tablespoons chopped onion
2 pounds fresh peas, shelled or 1½ cups tiny frozen peas, thawed
Salt to taste
4 cups homemade Chicken Stock (page 27) (½ cup less when using frozen peas)
1 cup raw short-grained pearl rice
3 tablespoons minced parsley
½ cup freshly grated Parmesan cheese

1. Melt butter in a saucepan and sauté onion over medium heat until transparent.

2. Add fresh peas and salt to taste. Sauté 2 minutes, then add 3 cups of the chicken stock. Cover and cook over low heat until peas are slightly cooked, about 5 to 10 minutes. (If using frozen peas, salt lightly, sauté 2 minutes, then add stock and bring to a quick boil.)

3. Add remaining stock, and stir in rice and parsley. Cover and cook over low heat, stirring occasionally, until rice is tender but firm to the bite, about 20 minutes. There should be a little liquid left. Taste and add salt if necessary.

4. Blend in freshly grated Parmesan cheese just before serving.

Makes 4 servings.

Menu suggestions. Serve before any fowl or meat dish. It is especially appropriate before Liver Venetian Style (page 58).

Bean and Pasta Soup (Pasta e Fagioli)

Typical of much Italian cookery is this hearty combination of beans and pasta.

1 cup dried white beans
Water
1 yellow onion, chopped
1 carrot, chopped
1 stalk celery, chopped
2 tablespoons minced parsley
1 clove garlic, minced
1 medium tomato, chopped
1 ham bone with some meat attached or 1 ham hock, cut into 3 pieces
2 cups homemade Beef Stock (page 27) or regular-strength canned beef broth
¾ cup any tubular macaroni
Salt and freshly ground pepper to taste
½ cup freshly grated Parmesan cheese

1. Cover beans with water and soak overnight. Drain.

2. In a stockpot, place beans, onion, carrot, celery, parsley, garlic, tomato, ham bone, and broth. Bring to boil over medium-high heat, reduce, cover, and simmer until beans are tender, about 2½ hours, adding water if necessary to maintain liquid level.

3. When beans are tender, take ½ cup and purée in food processor or put through a food mill. Return puréed beans to the stockpot.

4. Add macaroni and cook until tender but still quite firm to the bite, about 20 minutes. Season to taste with salt and pepper. Stir in freshly grated Parmesan cheese just prior to serving.

Makes 4 servings.

Menu suggestions. Such a hearty soup seems appropriate with simple meat dishes such as charcoal grilled steaks or sausages.

Cioppino is a variation of Italian fish soup that was developed by fishermen of Italian descent in California. A rich tomato broth is the essential ingredient, to which you can add whatever freshly caught fish or shellfish are available.

Fish Soup (Zuppa di Pesce)

Actually more like a stew than a soup, this hearty dish can be ready to eat in less than 30 minutes. Other kinds of fish can be substituted, according to what is available fresh from the market.

- ¼ **pound lean bacon** or pancetta, **diced**
- 1 **small onion, chopped**
- 1 **clove garlic, minced**
- 1 **cup chopped celery**
- ¼ **cup chopped green pepper**
- 4 **cups Italian-style plum tomatoes, peeled and cut into chunks** or **canned tomatoes, drained and cut into chunks.**
- 1 **cup Basic Tomato Sauce (page 36)** or **canned tomato sauce**
- 1 **cup water**
- 3 **medium potatoes, peeled and diced**
- 1½ **teaspoons salt**
- ⅛ **teaspoon pepper**
- ¼ **teaspoon dried oregano**
- ¼ **teaspoon dried basil**
- 1 **pound fresh halibut, cut into bite-sized pieces**
- ½ **pound sole, cut into bite-sized pieces**
- ½ **pound red snapper, cut into bite-sized pieces**
- 1 **cup dry white wine**
- 1 **tablespoon chopped fresh parsley**

1. In a large stockpot or Dutch oven, fry bacon until tender. Add onion, garlic, celery, and green pepper. Sauté until translucent.

2. Add tomatoes, tomato sauce, water, and potatoes. Cook over medium heat for 5 minutes. Add salt, pepper, oregano, and basil, cover, and simmer for 15 minutes.

3. Add fish and wine, cover, and continue simmering for 10 minutes. Sprinkle with chopped parsley before serving.

Makes 6 servings.

Menu suggestions. This soup is a meal in itself, and may be served with crusty French or Italian bread for dunking. Follow with a tossed green salad and a light dessert, such as one of the Fruit Ices (pages 90 to 91).

California Italian Fish Soup (Cioppino)

Italian-American fishermen of northern California are credited with inventing this tomato-based kettle of fish. Into the stock they tossed in the various catches of the day, allowing for much variety. Always serve accompanied by hot Garlic Bread (page 70) to dip into the broth.

- ½ **cup olive oil**
- 2 **yellow onions, finely chopped**
- 3 **cloves garlic, minced**
- 2 **cups Basic Tomato Sauce (page 36)** or **canned tomato sauce**
- 3 **cups coarsely chopped canned Italian-style plum tomatoes, along with their juice**
- 1 **tablespoon chopped fresh basil** or **1 teaspoon dried basil**
- 1 **tablespoon chopped fresh oregano** or **1 teaspoon dried oregano**
- **Salt and freshly ground black pepper to taste**
- 1 **pound shrimp, shelled and deveined**
- 2 **large or 4 small crabs, cleaned and cracked**
- 1 **pound firm-fleshed white fish filets, cut into bite-sized pieces**
- 12 **clams or mussels, well scrubbed**
- ½ **cup minced parsley**

1. In a large saucepan, heat olive oil over medium heat. Sauté onions until transparent, add garlic, and sauté 2 minutes more. Add tomato sauce, tomatoes, basil, oregano, salt, and pepper. Bring to a boil and cook 20 minutes, stirring occasionally.

2. Add fish and simmer until clams open, and fish is firm but tender and flakes easily, about 10 minutes. Correct seasonings and garnish with minced parsley.

Makes about 6 servings.

Menu suggestions. This hearty soup can be a one-dish meal, accompanied by garlic bread and followed by a crisp green tossed salad, with a simple dressing of olive oil and lemon juice. Serve in smaller portions as a first course before roast chicken or simple roasted meats. Do not serve it with tomato-based second courses.

Dried pasta, both imported and domestically made, comes in a vast array of sizes and shapes, often along with different names for similar sizes or shapes.

Pasta

People all over the world readily identify pasta as the highlight of Italian cooking. Spaghetti, macaroni, and ravioli are the best-known of innumerable varieties. Because of the regionalization of Italian cooking, names of pasta can be very confusing. Pasta going by the same name may appear in various shapes and sizes; likewise, pasta of the same shape and size may have several names.

The term *pasta asciutta* refers to dried pasta, such as spaghetti, *linguine*, and macaroni. *Pasta fresca* is freshly made pasta that is cooked or prepared without drying, such as *tortellini* and *fettucine*.

How to Cook Pasta

Choose a pasta cooker with a removable metal drainer, or use a large pot with a cover. For each pound of pasta to be cooked, bring 4 quarts of water to boil in a covered pot over high heat. When boiling, remove cover and add 1½ to 2 tablespoons salt.

Add pasta all at once, stirring thoroughly with a long-handled wooden spoon to keep pieces from sticking together. A tablespoon of cooking oil added to the boiling water also aids in keeping the strands separated. If dried strands (such as spaghetti) are too long to be totally immersed, drop them all into the water to whatever depth they will go. As the lower part softens with boiling, pasta will gradually bend and can

be pushed gently into the water with the spoon. Cover the pot to return the water to a rapid boil. When it is boiling, remove cover. Stir from time to time to prevent boiling over and sticking together.

The secret of good Italian pasta is to cook only until *al dente*—tender, but still firm to the bite. Do not overcook; pasta should never be limp and mushy. Each type of pasta needs a different cooking time, so the only way to know when pasta is done is to pull a piece out of the water and bite into it. Thin homemade noodles may be cooked in a matter of seconds; partially dried or packaged fresh noodles take about 2 to 3 minutes to cook; frozen pasta (which can go directly from the freezer to the water) about 3 minutes. Spaghetti and other dried macaroni products range from about 2 minutes for tiny soup *pastina* to as long as 15 minutes for *ziti*.

Good pasta should not sit around between the time it is done and the time it is served. *As soon as the noodles pass your taste test* remove from heat and drain immediately, either by pulling out the wire drainer from the pasta cooker or pouring the pasta into a large colander. Shake the drainer or colander rapidly several times in all directions to force out water. Immediately turn the pasta into a heated bowl for mixing, or into a serving dish to be topped with sauce. Add sauces, cheese, butter, and oil as directed in recipes, and toss quickly to coat all strands. Serve immediately while hot.

Good pasta must be cooked only until **al dente—** *tender, but still firm. Tasting is the only way to test for desired doneness. Drain pasta the moment it passes your taste test and pour immediately into a serving or mixing bowl. Toss to coat with oil or butter or selected sauce and serve as soon as possible.*

EATING PASTA TO STAY SLIM

Contrary to popular opinion, good Italian food does not have to be fattening. As with any other cuisine, it's primarily a matter of exercising comon sense when it comes to proportions. Today's Italian spas boast **cucina magra** (the Italian equivalent to France's **cuisine minceur**), which emphasizes simpler, lighter meals. But simpler and lighter need not mean blander and less interesting, as evidenced by the daily diet served in such spas: small portions of pasta, meat, and fish, lots of lightly cooked vegetables, and plenty of fresh fruits.

Such an idea is really nothing new to Italian eating habits. Although many courses are served, they are small; and fruit is a much more traditional Italian dessert than rich pastry.

How do such wonderful meals remain low in calories? The secret is in the sauce. Rich cream, sweet butter, and fresh cheese sauces obviously tip the caloric scales. But pasta, which—believe it or not—is low in calories, can be delicious with a simple, extremely low-calorie sauce made of fresh tomatoes, basil, garlic, a few drops of olive oil, and a light sprinkling of cheese. When choosing meats, low-calorie veal, chicken, and fish are natural favorites.

Basic Pasta (Pasta Fresca)

The ingredients are minimal, although preparation can be a bit tricky and time consuming until you get the hang of it. But the end results are heavenly, and once you've eaten the homemade version you'll find it difficult to return to dried noodles.

It is impossible to establish precise measurements for mixing pasta. Days vary in humidity, and eggs vary in size. The following recipe is based on large eggs, but you must learn to judge when the correct amount of flour has been added by how the dough feels. Practice makes perfect pasta.

Let's begin with the classic method of mixing, rolling, and cutting completely by hand.

To make Basic Pasta by hand, place eggs in a well of flour and beat lightly with a fork. Begin drawing flour into the eggs from the sides of the well with a circular motion. Toward the end of the mixing you'll probably decide to use your hands to blend the dough. Gather the mixed dough into a ball and set aside while you clean the work surface thoroughly of all bits of flour and egg.

2 cups flour
   (approximately)
3 eggs
1 teaspoon olive oil
½ teaspoon salt (optional)

1. Place flour in a mound on a smooth working surface. Make a well in the middle. Into this well put the eggs, oil, and salt. Beat the eggs lightly with a fork. Then, with a circular motion, begin to draw flour from the inside of the well—first with the fork, then with your fingers—incorporating the flour gradually into the eggs. Use one hand for mixing and the other to keep the wall of flour intact. When the eggs are no longer runny, push the flour over them and knead with both hands until a crumbly mass is formed. If it is sticky, gradually add a bit more flour. If it is dry, you may add a few drops of water or oil.

2. Place the dough to one side and clean the work surface of all scraps of flour and egg. Wash hands and lightly dust them and your work surface with flour. Replace the dough in the center of your work surface and knead

by pressing with palms of hands, folding over the dough and pressing again. Continue until dough is very elastic and smooth, and doesn't break off when you pull. This will take about 10 minutes or longer.

3. Clean the work surface and dust with more flour. Place the dough in the center, flatten with hands, and begin to roll out with a rolling pin, rolling away from you and picking up and turning dough as it flattens. Lightly dust work surface or top of dough with flour as required to keep it from sticking. Keep the dough shape as round as possible and roll to a thickness of about ⅛ inch.

4. When dough has been flattened to the correct thickness, begin to curl the far side of the dough around the rolling pin. As you pull the dough back and forth, move your cupped hands along the length of the pin to further stretch the dough in all directions. Work very quickly to prevent the dough from drying out, and turn it each time you repeat the rolling and stretching. You

should cover the entire sheet in less than 10 seconds, a total of 12 to 15 times around the circle. Dust with flour whenever the dough feels sticky. Roll and stretch until the dough is paper thin.

5. To make noodles, dust the dough well with flour and let it rest to dry for about 10 minutes. Then roll up like a jellyroll, flatten the top slightly, and cut with a sharp knife across the roll into desired widths: ¹⁄₁₆ inch for **tagliarini**; ⅛ inch for **fettuccine**; ¼ inch for **tagliatelle**.

6. After cutting the entire roll, open up the ribbons and spread noodles on a clean towel or waxed paper to dry (or hang noodles from a drying rack or dowel as described on page 17) about 5 minutes or so before cooking in boiling water as described on page 30.

If you are not going to cook them immediately, wrap in plastic wrap and refrigerate. Pasta will keep for a day or two this way. If you want to keep it longer, wrap in plastic wrap and freeze. You may also leave it to completely dry out at room temperature.

Store dried pasta in a cool, dry place, uncovered. It should keep about 4 to 6 weeks.

Other shapes. Wide **pappardelle** noodles are cut from the unrolled circle of dough with a knife or fluted pastry wheel, about ⅝ inch wide. Cut **lasagne** noodles the same way, about 1 inch wide. "Little squares," or **quadrucci**, cooked in broth, are made by first cutting the roll into **tagliatelle**, then cutting across the folded ribbons to make squares.

Dust your work surface lightly with flour and knead the pasta dough until smooth and elastic. If you wish, divide the kneaded dough into sections to make rolling easier. On a clean, flour-dusted surface roll the dough to a thickness of about ⅛ inch, turning the dough as you roll to keep it from sticking to the surface. Working as quickly as possible curl the dough around your rolling pin and stretch with cupped hands along the length of the pin as you simultaneously roll the dough back and forth. Allow the dough to dry for a few minutes, then roll it up jellyroll fashion and cut into desired shapes, such as fettuccini *as shown here. Or leave the dough flat and cut* pappardelle *noodles with a fluted pastry wheel.*

Basic Pasta (Pasta Fresca) **Made with a Pasta Machine**

Although connoisseurs hold out for completely handmade pasta, many cooks choose to use a pasta machine to speed the process along. The hand-cranked machine really requires two people for efficient operation: one person to feed and crank, and the other to catch the flattened dough. Although both the electric and nonelectric machines work on the same principle, the electric machine is much faster and can be easily operated by one person. Newer, more expensive pasta machines have compartments for mixing and kneading the dough automatically. Some versions have cutting disks to make tubular noodles as well as flat forms.

1. Mix dough as in Step 1 of Basic Pasta (page 32). Let dough rest, covered, about 1 hour, or until dry enough to go through the pasta machine without sticking.

2. Set the machine's smooth rollers at their widest opening and pull off a piece of dough about the size of a small lemon, or whatever size seems easiest for you to work with. Cover the rest of the dough to prevent drying. Feed the piece of dough through until it is very smooth and elastic, about 8 or 10 times. Each time the dough strip comes out, fold it in half before feeding it into the machine again. If dough gets sticky, dust lightly with flour.

3. Adjust roller to next setting and pass dough through, this time leaving the strip unfolded. Continue feeding the strip of dough through the rollers, narrowing the open-

ing down one step each time to thin out the dough to the desired degree (not **too** thin, though, or it will disintegrate when cooked). Pass dough through each of these settings about 2 or 3 times.

4. Repeat Steps 2 and 3 with each piece of dough until all dough has been processed. If making noodles, before cutting, spread out the strips to dry for about 15 minutes for wide noodles; longer for thin, spaghetti-like strands.

5. Adjust the blades to the proper cutting width. Put each dried strip of pasta through until cut, then hang or lay out to dry again, if necessary. (Pasta that is not dry enough will stick together in lumps when stored or cooked.) For larger noodle widths, follow directions for cutting by hand.

Both the hand-cranked and electric pasta machines are designed to make noodle preparation easier. The hand-cranked version (above) thins the dough to the desired thickness, then cuts it into selected widths. It works best if you have two pairs of hands, one to crank and feed and another to catch the noodles. An electric machine such as the one below can be operated by one cook. The machine completes the kneading operation as you feed in the dough, fold it over, and refeed. When the dough is smooth and elastic, the machine thins it to the desired thickness. Lay the strips to dry for a few minutes, then pass each strip through the selected cutting disc to quickly produce the desired width noodle.

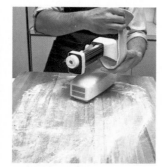
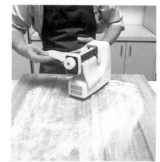

Satisfactory pasta dough can be mixed in a matter of seconds with food processors. If the bowl doesn't hold all the ingredients from either of our basic pasta dough recipes, divide in half, mix in the processor, then combine the dough pieces by hand. Cut by hand as shown on the preceding pages, or select one of the pasta machines illustrated on the opposite page.

Using the Food Processor to Mix Pasta Dough.

Although most good Italian cooks frown at mixing pasta dough by machine, it can be done, although admittedly not as well as by hand.

Position steel knife in processor bowl and add all ingredients in Basic Pasta (page 32) or Spinach Pasta recipes. Run machine until a ball is formed. Stop and check consistency. If sticky, add flour, 1 tablespoon at a time, and process until dough is smooth, about 40 seconds.

If your bowl will not hold all the ingredients in the basic recipes, place ½ of each ingredient in the bowl and process as above, repeating with second half (eggs can be beaten first in order to divide in half). Combine the two pieces by hand.

Proceed to roll dough by hand as in Step 3 of Basic Pasta, or put through the Pasta machine as directed.

Spinach Pasta (Pasta Verde)

Don't worry if the spinach creates spotty flecks as you begin kneading and rolling. By the time the dough is finished the pasta will be a smooth green. Spinach doesn't affect the taste of the pasta, but the dough will be softer than the yellow version.

½ **pound fresh spinach leaves, well washed** or ½ **10-ounce package frozen spinach, completely thawed**
½ **teaspoon salt**
2 **cups flour (approximately)**
2 **eggs**
1 **teaspoon olive oil (optional)**

1. Cook fresh spinach over medium heat in a covered pan, using only the water that clings to the leaves from washing. Add salt and cook until tender, about 10 minutes. (If using frozen spinach, thaw and cook with salt in a covered saucepan for about 5 minutes.) In either case, drain spinach well, squeeze dry with hands, and chop very fine **or** purée in the food processor or blender.

2. Shape flour into a mound, make a well, and add spinach, eggs, and oil in the well. Continue as directed in Steps 1 through 6 of Basic Pasta (page 32).

Makes about 6 servings.

Serving note. One of the showiest pasta presentations is known as "straw and hay" or **Paglia e Fieno**, a mixture of ½ spinach noodles with ½ regular yellow noodles tossed in butter and cream with freshly grated Parmesan cheese. The two pastas may also be tossed together in any light-colored sauce or fresh tomato sauce.

Pasta Sauces

Contrary to popular belief, not all pasta sauces include tomato, although it is an essential ingredient in many of them, particularly those of southern Italy.

Following is a sampling of sauces using a variety of ingredients. Actually, the range is endless. A sauce can be as simple and quick as melted butter and cheese, or as involved as a long-simmering ragù. One thing is certain: All pastas are enhanced by the addition of a good sauce.

The selection of a sauce should be dictated by the type of pasta being used. The thinner, finer noodles or small macaroni call for light sauces. Larger, heavier, or tubular types, which absorb sauce on both the outside and inside, take better to the thicker, more robust sauces.

Most good Italian cooks recommend that a little butter or olive oil be added to the hot pasta before pouring on the sauce. This improves the flavor and keeps the pasta from sticking together.

How much pasta to cook and how much sauce to add is really a matter of personal preference. As a general rule, ½ pound of raw pasta will make 3 medium-sized main dish servings, or 6 first course servings.

Basic Tomato Sauce (Salsa di Pomodoro)

This classic Italian sauce is suitable in all recipes calling for an all-purpose tomato sauce. When the summer garden is filled with ripe, tasty plum tomatoes, the wise cook prepares the sauce in quantity and cans or freezes it for use during the rest of the year. Use it in any recipe in this book that calls for tomato sauce; you'll find it far superior to the commercially canned variety.

2 cups canned Italian-style plum tomatoes or **2 pounds fresh plum tomatoes**
¼ **cup olive oil**
½ **cup chopped onion**
½ **cup chopped carrot**
½ **cup chopped celery**
1 **clove garlic, minced**
Salt to taste
½ **teaspoon sugar (optional)**

1. If using fresh tomatoes, peel, seed, and quarter them. Place in a covered pot and cook over medium heat for 10 minutes. For canned tomatoes, proceed to Step 2.

2. Heat oil in a saucepan and lightly brown onion, carrot, celery, and garlic. Stir in tomatoes, salt to taste, and sugar. Simmer gently for about 30 minutes or until thick.

3. Purée in food processor or blender, return to pan, and reheat before serving or preserving.

Makes about 2 cups sauce.

Variations. Fresh or dried herbs such as bay leaf, basil, or oregano may be added to taste.

White Sauce (Balsamella)

This predecessor of French **béchamel** is also called **Beschiamella**, and is used to bind filled pastas such as **cannelloni** and **lasagne**, and is the base for other additions in sauces for pasta and vegetables.

2 tablespoons butter
2 tablespoons flour
1 teaspoon salt
¼ **teaspoon white pepper**
2 cups milk

1. Melt butter in saucepan over medium-high heat. Tilt pan and stir in flour and seasonings. Blend well.

2. Add milk slowly and stir briskly with wooden spoon or wire whisk. Cook and stir continually over medium heat until boiling and thickened.

3. Remove from heat and use as described in various recipes.

Makes 2 cups.

Fresh Basil Sauce (Pesto)

Italian cooks labored long with mortar and pestle in hand to grind basil, pine nuts, and garlic into this redolent sauce. How grateful we should be for the food processor or blender!

Pesto is wonderful on pasta, and great in **Minestrone** (page 27), on baked potatoes, broiled fish, or spaghetti squash.

For the pasta course, use **Pesto** on homemade noodles, dried pasta, stuffed ravioli, or potato **gnocchi**.

The sauce can be made when basil is in season and frozen for longer storage in individual containers or plastic bags. To do this, drop small mounds onto a foil-covered cookie sheet. Freeze until firm, then package in a plastic bag, tightly wrapped. Thaw for 2 hours before serving, or place in a bowl of hot water for about 20 minutes before opening. **Never** make **Pesto** with dried basil.

2 cups firmly packed fresh basil leaves, washed and drained
¼ **cup pine nuts**
3 cloves garlic, peeled
¾ **cup freshly grated Parmesan cheese**
½ **cup olive oil**

1. Place basil, pine nuts, and garlic in blender or food processor and purée (or pound in mortar until puréed). Blend in cheese.

2. Slowly add oil until well mixed.

Note. To keep sauce from darkening until serving time, pour a thin layer of olive oil over the top of the sauce and store in refrigerator for up to three days.

Garbanzo Sauce (Salsa di Ceci)

Try this sauce over ½ pound small tubular or shell-type macaroni.

2 tablespoons olive oil
1 medium onion, chopped
1 large clove garlic, minced
2 cups peeled and quartered fresh or **canned Italian-style plum tomatoes**
3 anchovy filets
1 bay leaf
Pinch of saffron
Freshly ground black pepper to taste
2 cups canned garbanzo beans, drained
Chopped parsley for garnish

1. In large saucepan or 4-quart Dutch oven, place oil, onion, and garlic. Cook over medium heat until onion is softened, then add tomatoes, anchovy filets, bay leaf, saffron, and pepper. Simmer, uncovered, until sauce begins to thicken, about 30 to 45 minutes. Stir frequently.

2. Add the garbanzos and cook for an additional 10 minutes.

3. Place cooked macaroni in a large bowl and pour sauce over. Mix well and garnish with chopped parsley.

Makes 4 servings.

Fettuccine in Butter, Cream, and Cheese Sauce (Fettuccine all' Alfredo)

All you need to enjoy this dish are good cream, sweet butter, good quality Parmesan, and homemade noodles. Good fresh ingredients are the key, so try not to compromise. Dried fettuccine is a last resort. If you don't have time to make noodles yourself, fresh packaged noodles found in Italian delicatessens and some super markets are quite good.

½ cup sweet butter
1 cup heavy cream
    Homemade noodles
    (Basic Pasta recipe on
    page 32)
1 cup freshly grated
    Parmesan cheese
    Salt and freshly ground
    white pepper to taste
    Pinch of nutmeg

1. In a large heavy saucepan or casserole, melt the butter over low heat and add cream to heat through. Remove from heat while you cook the fettuccine as directed on page 30. Drain pasta and pour into pan with butter and cream.

2. Replace pan on very low heat and toss the noodles to coat well. Stir in the Parmesan and add salt and pepper to taste, along with a pinch of nutmeg. Mix quickly and serve immediately with a bowl of grated Parmesan to sprinkle on top.

Makes 4 to 6 servings.

Mushroom Sauce (Salsa al Funghi)

¼ pound pancetta or
    bacon or salt pork,
    diced
½ pound fresh mushrooms,
    sliced
¼ cup sliced green onions
1 6-ounce can tomato
    paste
1 cup water
½ teaspoon dried basil
½ teaspoon dried oregano
½ teaspoon sugar
¼ teaspoon salt
    Freshly ground black
    pepper to taste

1. In a 4-quart sauce pan or Dutch oven, cook diced pork over medium heat until browned, stirring frequently. Drain off excess fat. Add mushrooms and onion; cook until mushrooms are softened and lightly browned, stirring frequently.

2. Reduce heat and stir in tomato paste, water, herbs, sugar, salt and pepper. Cover and simmer gently 10 minutes.

3. Remove cover and continue to simmer over low heat until sauce thickens, about 30 minutes longer, stirring occasionally.

4. Serve over cooked spaghetti or other noodles with Parmesan cheese.

Makes enough sauce for ½ pound spaghetti, or 4 servings.

Spaghetti with Garlic and Oil (Spaghetti all' Aglio e Olio)

Romans are especially fond of this easily prepared, delicious dish. You'll find it a great late-night supper or first course Slow cooking of the garlic is the key to bringing out its sweetness. Always use the finest quality olive oil in this recipe. Serve over spaghetti or other thin, dried pasta.

¾ to 1 pound spaghetti
½ cup olive oil
1 tablespoon (or more)
    finely minced garlic
2 tablespoons chopped
    parsley
    Salt and freshly ground
    black pepper to taste

1. While water boils for spaghetti, heat oil in a small saucepan over low heat and very gently sauté garlic until golden. Turn off heat.

2. Cook spaghetti as directed on page 30. Drain and pour into large, preheated serving bowl. Toss quickly with garlic and oil. Add parsley, salt and pepper to taste. Serve immediately.

Makes 4 servings.

Fresh Basil and Tomato Sauce (Salsa alla Carrettiera)

An economical summer sauce with ingredients from your own Italian garden made in the spirit of the economy-minded cart drivers (carrettieri) of Rome, for whom the sauce is named.

Canned tomatoes are good substitutes for fresh, but there's no substitute for fresh basil. Serve over vermicelli, spaghettini, cappellini, or other thin, dried pasta.

1 to 1½ cups cleaned,
    washed, and chopped
    fresh basil leaves
2 cups peeled, seeded,
    and chopped fresh or
    canned Italian-style
    plum tomatoes (drain
    canned variety)
4 teaspoons minced garlic
½ cup olive oil
    Salt and freshly ground
    black pepper to taste

1. Combine basil, tomatoes, and garlic in a saucepan and cook in olive oil over medium heat for about 15 to 18 minutes. Add salt and pepper to taste. Remove from heat.

2. Cook pasta according to directions on page 30, drain, and pour into heated bowl. Toss with the sauce and serve immediately.

Makes 4 servings.

Menu suggestions. Fried Cheese (page 24) is a good way to start off. The basil-rich sauce is excellent before any roasted meats. Avoid dishes that use a lot of tomatoes.

Butter Sauce (Salsa al Burro)

This is the easiest sauce to make for homemade noodles, and it is compatible with anything you put on your menu.

½ cup sweet butter, melted
1 cup freshly grated
    Parmesan cheese
    Salt and freshly ground
    black pepper to taste

1. Cook pasta according to directions on page 30. Drain and transfer to heated serving bowl.

2. Mix butter with the pasta. Add ½ the cheese and season with salt and pepper to taste. Serve immediately. Pass remaining cheese in a bowl at the table for diners to sprinkle on pasta.

Makes 4 servings.

Eggplant Sauce (Salsa con le Melanzone)

1 medium-sized eggplant
    (about 1 pound), pared
    and cut into 1-inch
    cubes
2 tablespoons flour
½ cup olive oil
½ cup sliced onion
2 cups fresh peeled
    and quartered plum
    tomatoes or 1 1-pound
    can Italian-style plum
    tomatoes, quartered,
    and drained
6 ounces tomato purée
½ teaspoon salt
1 teaspoon dried basil
    Freshly ground black
    pepper to taste
¼ teaspoon sugar
    Freshly grated
    Parmesan cheese

1. Sprinkle eggplant cubes with flour and toss to coat well; set aside.

2. In a 4-quart saucepan or Dutch oven, heat oil and add prepared eggplant cubes. Brown lightly, stirring frequently. Remove to absorbent paper to drain.

3. Place onion in pot, adding more oil if necessary, and cook until lightly browned. Stir in tomatoes, tomato purée, salt, basil, pepper, and sugar. Boil gently, uncovered, for 20 minutes, stirring occasionally. Add eggplant and boil gently, covered, 15 to 20 minutes longer, or until eggplant is fork tender.

4. Serve over cooked spaghetti or other pasta with Parmesan cheese

Makes 4 to 6 servings, or, enough for ¾ to 1 pound spaghetti.

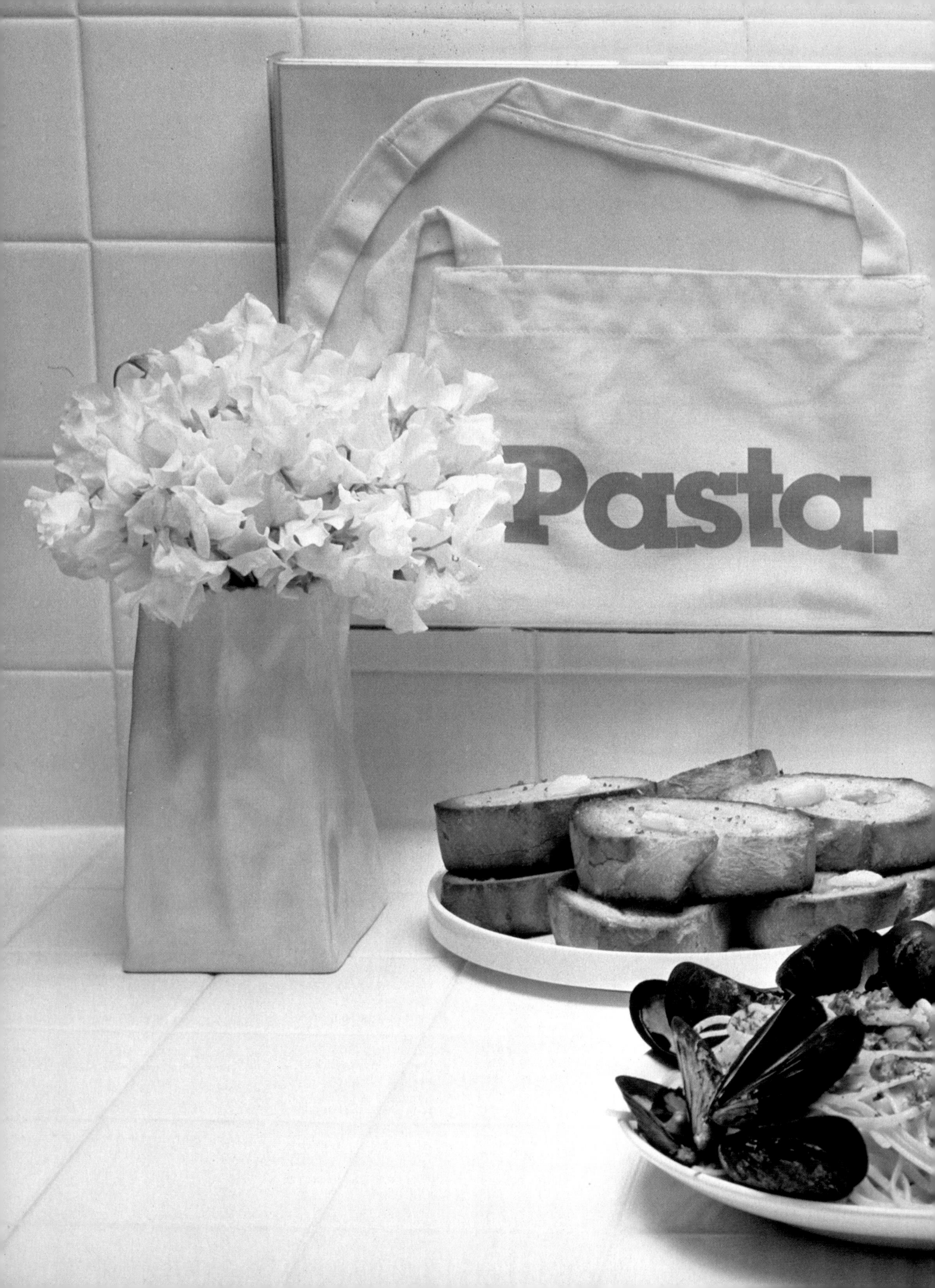
Pasta.

Mussels make a showy variation of Clam Sauce (recipe on page 40). Prepare them in the same way as the clams, removing some of the meat from the shells or leaving them all intact as shown here. Toss the pasta with the remaining ingredients and arrange the steamed mussels on top. In Italy grated cheese is never served with any seafood pasta sauce; however Americans often enjoy a sprinkling of Parmesan or other cheese. Garlic Bread (recipe on page 70) is the traditional accompaniment for soaking up the sauce.

Substitutions and variations based on available ingredients are the very heart of Italian home cooking. For a vegetarian pasta course, prepare Canneloni (recipe on page 47), substituting a mixture of drained chopped spinach with ricotta cheese and your favorite seasonings for the filling.

White Clam or Mussel Sauce (Salsa alle Vongole)

Select the smallest clams available to capture the flavor of **vongole** from the Mediterranean. The texture and flavor of canned imports from the Orient prove more authentic than our fresh cherrystone clams. Fresh mussels are even more flavorful and make a showy presentation when arranged atop linguine as shown in the photo on pages 38-39. **Linguine** is classic for this sauce, but you may serve it over 1 pound of any thin, dried pasta.

Seafood Sauce (Salsa Marinara)

This quickly prepared sauce blends the flavors of the Italian garden with those of the sea.

2 cups minced onion
½ cup olive oil
4 cloves garlic, minced or pressed
1 cup dry white wine
3 cups seeded and drained canned Italian-style plum tomatoes
¼ cup chopped fresh basil or **4 teaspoons dried basil**
1 tablespoon dried oregano
½ cup chopped parsley
3 pounds small fresh clams, well scrubbed or **3 6½-ounce cans small clams**
2 pounds scallops, quartered
2 pounds shrimp, peeled and deveined
Salt and freshly ground black pepper to taste

1. Sauté onion in olive oil over medium-high heat until golden. Add garlic and sauté 30 seconds more. Pour in wine and cook until evaporated, about 2 minutes.

2. Add tomatoes and herbs. Increase heat and boil for about 5 minutes, then reduce heat to simmer. Cook for 30 to 45 minutes, until sauce is slightly thickened.

3. Add fresh clams, cover, and cook until shells open, about 5 minutes. (Add canned clams at same time as shrimp and scallops.)

4. Add scallops and shrimp. Cover and cook until barely firm, about 3 minutes. Add salt and pepper to taste. Remove from heat and toss with pasta in heated bowl. If sauce must be held, quickly reheat just before serving time.

Makes about 12 servings.

2 pounds fresh clams or mussels or **2 6½-ounce cans chopped clams and their juice**
¼ cup olive oil
2 cloves garlic
⅓ cup dry white wine
Freshly ground black pepper to taste
2 tablespoons parsley, chopped

1. If using canned clams, begin with Step 2. If using fresh clams or mussels, scrub thoroughly with a stiff brush to remove any specks of sand or barnacles. Place clams or mussels in a colander and set in a large pot containing approximately 2 inches of boiling water. Cover with a tight-fitting lid and steam just until shells begin to open. Remove a few shells with meat inside, and reserve for garnish. Then remove the meat from the rest of the shells. Dice meat and set aside. Strain the

juice from the pan through a paper coffee filter, cheese cloth, or fine sieve; reserve ½ cup liquid.

2. Heat 3 tablespoons olive oil over medium heat, add garlic cloves and brown them lightly to flavor the oil, then discard garlic.

3. Add cooked fresh clams or mussels or canned clams, along with their juice and the white wine. Cook over medium-high heat for about 2 minutes, or until half of the liquid has evaporated. Add pepper to taste and the parsley, or fresh parsley can be sprinkled on pasta when tossed with clam sauce to add color. Simmer for 4 to 5 minutes.

4. Meanwhile, cook **linguine** according to directions on page 30. Drain and place in serving dish, cover with clam sauce, and toss gently. Garnish with reserved clams or mussels in the shell and serve immediately.

Makes 4 servings.

Oyster Sauce (Salsa di Ostriche)

Serve this over ½ pound spaghetti, **linguine**, or other thin, dried pasta.

- 1½ cups canned or fresh small oysters, with their juice
- 2 cloves garlic, minced
- ¼ cup finely chopped onion
- 2 tablespoons olive oil
- 2 tablespoons butter White wine
- ¼ cup finely chopped parsley
- ¼ teaspoon dried basil Salt and freshly ground black pepper to taste

1. If oysters are not extra-small, chop them into smaller pieces.

2. Sauté garlic and onion in oil and butter until golden.

3. Measure juices from oysters and add wine to make 1 cup total liquid. Add to onion and garlic mixture and simmer for 5 minutes. Add parsley, basil, and salt and pepper to taste.

4. Add oysters and simmer 2 to 3 minutes.

Makes 4 servings.

Tuna Sauce (Salsa al Tonno)

- ½ cup finely chopped onion
- ¼ cup olive oil
- 2 cloves garlic, minced
- 2 tablespoons chopped parsley
- 2 tablespoons dried basil
- 1 cup chopped fresh or canned Italian-style plum tomatoes
- 1 7-ounce can tuna packed in olive oil, drained or tuna packed in water, drained, marinated in olive oil, and drained again
- 1 tablespoon tiny capers Salt and freshly ground black pepper to taste

1. Sauté onion in olive oil until soft, add garlic, and sauté until lightly golden. Add parsley and tomatoes and simmer about 20 minutes.

2. As sauce simmers, cook pasta until al dente.

3. About 5 minutes before the pasta is ready, add tuna and capers to the simmering sauce. Taste and add salt and pepper.

4. Drain pasta and transfer to heated bowl. Toss with sauce and serve.

Makes 4 to 6 servings, when served over 1 pound spaghetti or other pasta.

Menu suggestions. As part of a typically all-fish dinner, follow with any grilled or sautéed fish. Do not serve with dishes containing tomato sauces.

Crabmeat Sauce (Salsa di Granchi)

Serve over ¾ to 1 pound spaghetti, **linguine**, or other thin, dried pasta.

- 2 tablespoons olive oil
- ½ cup coarsely chopped onion
- 3 cups peeled and quartered fresh tomatoes or 1 1-pound, 12-ounce can Italian-style plum tomatoes
- 2 tablespoons chopped parsley
- 1 large bay leaf
- ½ teaspoon salt Freshly ground black pepper to taste
- ¼ cup dry white wine
- ½ pound cooked crab, flaked

1. Heat oil in a 4-quart saucepan, over medium heat. Add onion and cook until lightly browned. Stir in tomatoes, parsley, bay leaf, salt, and pepper. Cover and boil gently for 15 minutes.

2. Add wine and boil gently, uncovered, for 30 minutes, stirring occasionally.

3. Remove bay leaf; add crabmeat and cook gently for 5 to 10 minutes, until crab is heated through.

Makes 4 to 6 servings, or enough sauce for ¾ to 1 pound spaghetti.

Shrimp Sauce (Salsa di Scampi)

Serve over ¾ to 1 pound spaghetti or other thin, dried pasta.

- 2 tablespoons olive oil
- ⅓ cup coarsely chopped celery
- ¼ cup very finely minced onion
- 1 clove garlic, finely minced
- 3 cups peeled and quartered fresh tomatoes or 1 1-pound 12-ounce can Italian-style plum tomatoes, chopped and drained.
- 6 ounces tomato paste
- ½ teaspoon salt
- ½ teaspoon dried basil
- ¼ teaspoon dried oregano
- ¼ teaspoon dried thyme Freshly ground black pepper to taste
- 1½ pounds fresh or frozen shrimp, shelled and deveined

1. In a large saucepan, heat oil. Add celery, onion, and garlic; cook until just tender but still crisp. Stir in tomatoes, tomato paste, salt, herbs, and pepper. Cover and simmer gently 15 minutes.

2. Uncover and boil gently for 30 minutes or until sauce thickens, stirring occasionally. Add shrimp and boil, covered, 5 minutes longer or until shrimp are cooked.

3. Serve over cooked spaghetti or noodles.

Makes 4 to 6 servings, or enough sauce for ¾ to 1 pound spaghetti.

Variation. Fresh scallops, cut into quarters, can be substituted for part or all of the shrimp.

Pasta with Peas and Prosciutto (Pasta con Piselli alla Romana)

Springtime visitors to Rome enjoy tender fresh peas sautéed with **prosciutto**. Harvest your own young peas for truly authentic Italian cooking, select young market peas in season, or use frozen tiny peas anytime. Serve over **fettuccine** or other noodles.

- 1 cup shredded prosciutto
- 2 tablespoons butter
- 1 cup tiny peas, thawed if frozen
- ½ cup butter
- ½ cup heavy cream
- 1 cup freshly grated Parmesan cheese
- ½ cup parsley, minced Salt, freshly ground nutmeg, and freshly ground white pepper to taste

1. In a skillet over medium, heat, sauté **prosciutto** in 2 tablespoons of butter until translucent. Add peas and continue cooking until peas are just tender, about 5 minutes. Remove from heat and set aside.

2. While pasta cooks, melt ½ cup butter with cream over very low heat. Do not allow to boil.

3. Drain pasta, pour into large bowl, and toss with butter and cream. Add cheese and mix well, then quickly stir in parsley, salt, nutmeg, pepper, and the peas and **prosciutto**. Serve immediately.

Makes 4 to 6 servings.

When fresh spring peas are not available, frozen tiny peas are a perfectly acceptable substitute in Pasta with Peas and Prosciutto. Ingredients may be combined with freshly drained pasta at the table for a showy presentation.

Northern Italian Meat Sauce (Ragù alla Bolognese)

It would be impossible to give a single recipe for the classic Italian meat sauce, **ragù**. Every cook has his or her own version. We offer here three of the best that we found. The first two are basically tomato sauces, one of which has more herbs and seasonings than the other. The third is a creamier sauce, with a subtle hint of lemon. We recommend the first two be used with any pasta—spaghetti, noodles, or one of the filled pastas such as ravioli. They may also be used in baked **lasagne**. Version III, because it is a thicker, richer sauce, combines best with spaghetti, homemade noodles, or one of the large tube-type macaroni such as **rigatoni**.

Ragù alla Bolognese, Version I

- **1 tablespoon olive oil**
- **2 tablespoons butter**
- **½ cup diced lean salt pork** or pancetta or **bacon**
- **¼ cup finely chopped yellow onion**
- **¼ cup finely chopped carrot**
- **¼ cup finely chopped celery**
- **2 to 3 chicken livers, finely chopped** (optional)
- **1 pound lean ground beef**
- **½ cup dry white wine**
- **4 cups chopped canned Italian-style plum tomatoes, with juice Salt and freshly ground black pepper to taste**
- **1 bay leaf**
- **½ teaspoon dry basil**
- **½ teaspoon dry oregano**
- **4 tablespoons milk** or **light cream**

1. Heat oil and 1 tablespoon butter in a 4-quart saucepan or Dutch oven. Add pork and sauté until tender. Add onion, carrot, and celery and cook until vegetables are wilted, about 2 minutes.

2. Add chicken livers and ground beef, breaking up with a wooden spoon, and cook until meat turns light brown. Add wine and cook until liquid evaporates, about 5 minutes.

3. Pour in tomatoes and cook over medium heat until mixture starts to bubble, stirring frequently. Add salt, pepper, bay leaf, basil, and oregano. Reduce heat to simmer, cover and cook slowly for 2 hours, stirring occasionally.

4. Add remaining 1 tablespoon butter, and milk or cream, and stir until thoroughly mixed into the sauce. Adjust seasoning if necessary.

Makes 2 quarts.

Ragu sauce in the style of Bologna is the perfect topping for freshly made green tagliarini *noodles from the recipe on page 35.*

Ragù alla Bolognese, Version II

- **3 tablespoons olive oil**
- **1 large onion, chopped**
- **1 clove garlic, minced**
- **½ cup finely chopped bell pepper**
- **½ cup finely chopped carrots**
- **¼ pound fresh mushrooms, sliced**
- **¼ cup chopped fresh parsley**
- **½ pound ground beef**
- **1 16-ounce can tomato purée**
- **2 8-ounce cans tomato sauce**
- **½ cup dry red wine**
- **1 teaspoon dried oregano**
- **¼ teaspoon dried leaf thyme**
- **½ teaspoon dried basil**
- **1 tablespoon salt**
- **½ teaspoon pepper**
- **1 teaspoon sugar**
- **1 bay leaf**

1. Heat oil in a 4-quart saucepan or Dutch oven. Add onion, garlic, bell pepper, carrots, mushrooms, and parsley. Sauté over medium heat until vegetables are wilted.

2. Add ground beef, breaking up with a wooden spoon, and cook until meat turns light brown. Add all remaining ingredients. Continue to cook over medium heat until sauce starts to bubble. Lower heat to simmer, cover, and cook for 2 hours, stirring occasionally.

3. Remove cover, adjust seasoning if necessary, and continue to cook for an additional 15 to 20 minutes or until thickened.

Makes 2 quarts.

Ragù alla Bolognese, Version III

- **¼ pound minced bacon** or prosciutto
- **1 tablespoon butter**
- **½ cup chopped carrots**
- **½ cup chopped celery**
- **½ cup chopped onions**
- **½ pound lean ground beef**
- **2 or 3 chicken livers, chopped**
- **1 tablespoon tomato paste**
- **½ cup dry white wine**
- **1 cup beef bouillon Salt and freshly ground black pepper to taste**
- **⅛ teaspoon ground nutmeg**
- **1 teaspoon grated lemon rind**
- **½ cup heavy cream**

1. In a heavy 4-quart saucepan or Dutch oven, cook bacon in butter until soft and golden. Add carrot, celery, and onion. Cook over low heat until tender.

2. Add beef and brown evenly. Add chicken livers and cook for 2 or 3 minutes. Stir in tomato paste and wine, and cook for another 2 minutes. Add bouillon, salt and pepper to taste, nutmeg, and lemon rind.

3. Simmer, covered, over low heat for 40 minutes. Before serving, heat cream but do not boil. Stir into sauce.

Makes enough sauce for ¾ to 1 pound spaghetti or other pasta.

Norma's Meat Sauce

This economical tomato-based sauce keeps well in the refrigerator for up to five days, or in the freezer for about four months. You may want to double or triple the recipe to make the long simmering time more worthwhile.

- **1 pound lean ground beef**
- **1 teaspoon thyme**
- **1 teaspoon salt**
- **½ teaspoon freshly ground black pepper**
- **3 cups basic Tomato Sauce (page 36) or canned tomato sauce**
- **3 cups water**
- **2 cloves garlic, halved**
- **1 bay leaf**
- **4 ounces fresh mushrooms, diced**
- **1 teaspoon sugar**
- **¾ teaspoon cinnamon**

1. Brown ground beef in skillet over high heat. With slotted spoon, transfer meat to heavy 2-quart saucepan. Add thyme, salt, pepper, tomato sauce, water, garlic, and bay leaf. Bring to boil and reduce heat to low.

2. Cover and simmer for 4 to 5 hours, stirring occasionally. (If sauce appears too thick toward end of cooking time, add a little water.)

3. One hour before serving time, add mushrooms, sugar, and cinnamon, and continue simmering. Remove bay leaf and garlic before serving.

Makes 3 to 4 cups.

Menu suggestions. Serve over spaghetti, ravioli, or thin **polenta** (page 52). Top with freshly grated Parmesan or **romano** cheese. Excellent sauce for southern Italian-style **lasagne**.

Spaghetti Sauce with Italian Sausage (Salsicce in Umido)

The rich flavor of Italian sausage needs no assistance from sauces or vegetables. However, its unmistakable flavor turns spaghetti sauce into a savory Italian delight. Although this recipe calls for the mild sweet sausages, use the hot ones if you prefer a spicier sauce, or mix half-and-half.

- **1 pound Italian sausage, hot or sweet**
- **¼ cup hot water**
- **½ pound fresh mushrooms, sliced**
- **½ cup shredded carrot**
- **1 medium onion, sliced**
- **½ cup chopped celery**
- **¼ cup minced parsley**
- **1 1-pound, 12-ounce can Italian-style plum tomatoes**
- **6 ounces tomato paste**
- **1 cup dry red wine**
- **1 bay leaf**
- **2 teaspoons salt**
- **1 teaspoon dried basil Freshly ground black pepper to taste**

1. Prick Italian sausage casings and place in a cold skillet. Pour hot water over them, cover, and cook for 10 minutes. Remove sausages with slotted spoon and cut into 1½-inch chunks.

2. Pour sausage drippings into a large Dutch oven and sauté mushrooms, carrots, onion, celery, and parsley until just tender but still crisp. Drain off any excess fat and return sausages to pot.

3. Add tomatoes, tomato paste, wine, bay leaf, salt, basil, and pepper. Cover and simmer 1½ hours or until thickened, stirring occasionally. Taste to correct seasoning.

Makes 1½ quarts.

Italian dining at home is easy if you have Italian markets nearby. Fresh pasta (left) *needs only a simple sauce of butter and cheese. Sausages* (right) *can be quickly transformed from one of the accompanying recipes.*

Spaghetti Sauce with Meatballs (Polpette al Sugo)

Meatballs (Polpette)
- **1 pound lean ground beef**
- **¼ pound ground pork**
- **2 slices firm white bread**
- **½ cup milk**
- **¾ cup finely chopped onion**
- **½ teaspoon dried oregano**
- **¼ cup grated Parmesan cheese**
- **¼ cup finely minced parsley**
- **1 egg, lightly beaten Salt and freshly ground black pepper to taste**

1. Combine beef and pork in a large bowl. Soak bread in milk for 10 minutes, drain off excess milk.

2. Add milk-soaked bread to meat, together with all remaining ingredients. Mix thoroughly. Shape into 18 to 20 meatballs, each about 2 inches in diameter.

3. Arrange meatballs on an oiled broiling tray. Broil under high heat, turning carefully with a spatula so that meatballs do not break.

4. When meatballs are brown on all sides, remove from baking sheet and drop into prepared sauce (recipe below). Simmer gently for 30 to 45 minutes.

Sauce (Sugo)
- **1 cup chopped onion**
- **2 tablespoons olive oil**
- **1 clove garlic, minced**
- **2 tablespoons minced parsley**
- **3 cups peeled and quartered fresh tomatoes, or 1 1-pound, 12-ounce can Italian-style plum tomatoes**
- **1 teaspoon oregano Salt and freshly ground black pepper to taste**
- **½ cup dry red wine**

1. Sauté onion in olive oil until tender. Add garlic. Simmer 3 to 4 minutes, then add parsley, tomatoes, oregano, salt, and pepper. Cover and cook over low heat for 20 minutes.

2. Add cooked meatballs and continue to cook as directed in Step 4 of Meatball recipe. Add wine during last 10 minutes of cooking.

Makes 6 to 8 servings when served over cooked spaghetti or noodles.

Chicken Liver Sauce (Fegatini al Sugo)

- **¼ cup olive oil**
- **1 pound chicken livers, cut into bite-sized pieces**
- **1 medium onion, sliced**
- **½ cup diced green pepper**
- **3 cups peeled and quartered fresh tomatoes or 1 1-pound, 12-ounce can Italian-style plum tomatoes**
- **1 teaspoon salt Freshly ground black pepper to taste**
- **½ teaspoon dried marjoram**
- **½ cup dry white wine Freshly grated Parmesan cheese**

1. In a saucepan over medium-high heat, combine oil and chicken livers and cook until lightly browned, about 3 minutes, stirring frequently.

Remove livers with a slotted spoon and set aside.

2. Reduce heat and add onion and green pepper and cook until lightly browned. Stir in tomatoes, salt, pepper, and marjoram. Simmer gently, uncovered, for 30 minutes, stirring occasionally.

3. Add browned livers, cover, and simmer 15 minutes longer. Add wine and simmer an additional 10 minutes.

4. Serve over cooked spaghetti or other pasta with a sprinkling of grated Parmesan.

Makes 4 to 6 servings, or enough sauce for ¾ to 1 pound pasta.

Spaghetti Charcoal Maker's Style (Spaghetti alla Carbonara)

There's no charcoal in this recipe—the name comes from Rome, where this hearty sauce was a special favorite of coal workers.

- **1 cup diced** pancetta or **bacon** or **cooked ham**
- **3 tablespoons olive oil**
- **4 tablespoons butter**
- **¾ pound spaghetti**
- **4 egg yolks at room temperature, well beaten**
- **1 cup freshly grated Parmesan cheese**
- **½ cup heavy cream Salt and freshly ground black pepper to taste**
- **¼ cup minced parsley**

1. Sauté **pancetta** or other pork product in 2 tablespoons olive oil until meat is translucent. Reduce heat, add butter, melt, and reserve.

2. While spaghetti cooks, beat together egg yolks, 1 tablespoon olive oil, Parmesan cheese, cream, salt, and a generous amount of pepper. Combine with pork and cooled butter.

3. Drain pasta and turn into serving bowl. Stir in bacon and egg mixture, along with parsley, and mix until spaghetti is thoroughly coated. Serve immediately, with a bowl of Parmesan cheese for diners to sprinkle on pasta.

Makes 4 to 6 servings.

Menu suggestions. Almost a meal in itself, **Spaghetti alla Carbonara** is a hearty lunch or quick supper when teamed with a crisp tossed salad. If you want a second course, choose any simple meat dish such as Veal Cutlet Milan Style, page 56, or fried chicken.

Stuffed Pasta

The only stuffed pasta most Americans have ever eaten is ravioli and lasagne. But there are a variety of stuffings (chicken, cheese, meat) and a variety of shapes (*tortellini, cappelletti, cannelloni*) from which to choose.

Using a ravioli pin is authentic and fun. Spread selected filling on a sheet of green or white pasta dough, then cover with a second sheet. Roll the pin over the top sheet to create squares formed by the indentations in the pin. Finally, cut the squares apart with a sharp knife or pastry wheel.

Stuffed Pasta Rings (Tortellini)

Little round **tortellini** may be cooked in water, drained, and served in butter and cream, basil and garlic, tomato or meat sauce. They may be also cooked directly in chicken or meat broth and served in the soup.

Homemade Basic Pasta or **Spinach Pasta (page 32 or 35), with 1 tablespoon milk added**
Filling: Choose either Chicken Filling, Herbed Cheese Filling, or Meat and Cheese Filling, or Sausage Filling
Water or broth for cooking

1. Combine milk with eggs and prepare dough according to directions. After rolling out the completed dough (either by hand or with the pasta machine), cut into 2-inch circles with a floured biscuit cutter or glass.

2. Prepare one of the stuffing mixtures that follow, and place about ½ teaspoon (according to actual size of circles) in the center of each piece. Fold the circle of pasta over in half so that the edge of the top half does not quite meet the edge of the bottom half. Press and seal tightly with fingers. Pick up the half-moon shape and wrap it around your finger, with the rounded side upward. Press one corner over the other end, and gently press tips together to form a circle. If they don't stick, moisten corners with a dab of water and press again. Cover pasta to keep from drying out while assembling.

3. Place stuffed **tortellini** in rows on a clean towel. Cook immediately, or turn them every 2 hours to dry on all sides. Place dried tortellini in an uncovered bowl and store up to a week in a cool dry place, or in the refrigerator. They may also be wrapped tightly in plastic wrap, and frozen.

4. To cook **tortellini** in water, bring 4 quarts of water to a boil. Stir in 2 tablespoons salt and drop in **tortellini**, stirring from time to time to prevent sticking. After water returns to a boil, cook until tender —about 5 to 8 minutes for fresh pasta, 15 to 20 minutes for dried pasta, and up to 25 minutes for frozen pasta. Drain well, place in preheated bowl, and toss with heated sauce.

Makes about 150 **tortellini**. (Allow about 24 **tortellini** per serving.)

Variations. Tortellini are delicious tossed in butter and cream, as in **Tortellini** in Cream. Or cook and serve in broth as in **Tortellini in Brodo**.

Tortellini is formed by filling pasta rounds with any chosen stuffing mixture and folding the dough over to seal. Wrap the half-moon shape around your finger and press the ends together to form little rings.

Four Fillings for Small Stuffed Pasta: Tortellini, **Ravioli**, Cappelletti

Choose from these or create your own from available cooked meats or vegetables on hand. Simply combine all ingredients and mix well. Correct the seasonings to your taste.

Chicken Filling

- **2 cups finely chopped cooked chicken breast**
- **½ cup freshly grated Parmesan cheese**
- **1 tablespoon minced parsley**
- **1 egg yolk, lightly beaten**
- **2 tablespoons butter, melted**
- **Salt and freshly ground nutmeg and white pepper to taste**

Meat and Cheese Filling

- **½ cup ground veal**
- **½ cup ground pork**
- **1 cooked chicken breast, finely chopped**
- **2 slices** mortadella or prosciutto, **finely chopped**
- **1 cup freshly grated Parmesan cheese**
- **2 tablespoons chopped parsley**
- **Salt and freshly ground black pepper to taste**

Sausage Filling

- **3 tablespoons minced onion, sauteed until soft in 1 tablespoon butter**
- **1 pound sweet Italian sausage, casing removed, crumbled and sautéed with the onion until cooked through**
- **⅓ cup dry bread crumbs**
- **2 egg yolks, beaten**
- **3 tablespoons freshly grated Parmesan cheese**
- **Salt and freshly ground black pepper to taste**

Herbed Cheese Filling

- **1½ cups** ricotta **cheese**
- **1 cup freshly grated Parmesan cheese**
- **½ cup chopped parsley**
- **1 teaspoon dried basil** or oregano, **crumbled**
- **1 egg yolk, lightly beaten**
- **Salt and freshly ground nutmeg to taste**

Tortellini **in Cream** (Tortellini alla Panna)

Egg yolks added to thick cream create an elegant and rich sauce for either homemade or frozen **tortellini**.

- **24 ounces homemade** tortellini or **purchased frozen**
- **2 cups heavy cream**
- **¼ cup butter**
- **3 egg yolks**
- **1 cup freshly grated Parmesan cheese**
- **Freshly ground nutmeg and white pepper to taste**
- **Fresh minced parsley for garnish**

1. Cook **tortellini** as directed in recipe or on package.

2. Heat butter and cream until butter is melted. Pour a small amount of the mixture into the egg yolks, combine well, then pour egg yolk mixture back into the hot cream and stir over low heat only until sauce begins to thicken.

3. Add grated Parmesan cheese, nutmeg, and white pepper to taste. Combine well and serve immediately, garnished with parsley.

Makes 8 servings.

Tortellini in Broth (Tortellini in Brodo)

- **2½ quarts homemade Chicken or Meat Broth (page 27)** or **regular-strength canned broth**
  Tortellini, **½ the recipe** or **about 15 to 18 per serving**
- **¼ cup chopped parsley**
  Freshly grated Parmesan cheese

1. Bring broth to a boil. Drop in **tortellini** and stir to keep from sticking. Cook until **al dente**, according to directions on page 30.

2. Ladle into bowls, sprinkle with parsley, and pass Parmesan cheese at the table.

Makes 6 servings.

Menu suggestions. This dish can go with any appetizer or second course.

Stuffed Pasta Squares (Ravioli)

Almost as popular as spaghetti, these filled squares may contain almost any stuffing mixture the cook can dream up and may be served with any sauce you choose.

Basic Pasta or **Spinach Pasta (page 32 or page 35), with 1 tablespoon milk added to the eggs**
Filling: Choose either Chicken Filling (page 45) or **Herbed Cheese Filling,** or **Meat and Cheese Filling,** or **Sausage Filling**
1 egg, beaten

1. Roll out half the dough until it is a thin sheet. Place mounded teaspoons of filling in even rows, like a checkerboard, on top of the dough. Roll out the remaining dough, brush with egg, and place the sheet egg-covered-side down over the top of the filling-patterned pasta. Press down firmly around the mounds of filling.

2. Cut the pasta into squares along horizontal and vertical lines between the mounds with a ravioli cutter, sharp knife, or fluted pastry wheel. Separate squares and set aside on clean towel.

3. Cook in 4 quarts boiling salted water. Gently stir with long-handled wooden spoon to keep from sticking. Cook until **al dente**, about 5 to 10 minutes. Drain and turn into a heated bowl containing melted butter or some of the sauce. Toss gently to coat all sides, add more sauce, and serve.

Makes about 6 servings.

Using the ravioli pin. Instead of mounds, spread filling smoothly over the bottom layer, then add the egg-brushed top. Roll the wooden, indented ravioli pin across the top layer vertically and horizontally in a checkerboard pattern. This will firmly seal layers together and imprint the cutting lines. Then cut with pastry wheel or knife to separate the squares.

An alternative to making ravioli with a pin, as shown on page 44, calls for rolling two rectangles of pasta dough, either green or white, and dotting with dollops of the selected filling. Brush the top piece with beaten egg and place coated side down over the filled piece. Press the top layer firmly around the mounds of filling to seal. Cut with a knife or pastry wheel to form squares.

Baked Lasagne with Meat Sauce (Lasagne al Ragù)

This northern Italian version of **lasagne** is especially light, compared to the tomato-heavy **lasagne** most Americans are familiar with. Prepare with homemade noodles for a real treat.

Basic Pasta or **Spinach Pasta (page 32** or **page 35)** or **1 pound dried** lasagne **noodles**
6 cups Northern Italian Meat Sauce, Version I or **II (page 42)**
About **4 cups White Sauce, double the recipe on page 36**
2 cups freshly grated Parmesan cheese
¼ cup butter

1. Prepare pasta and cut into strips about 4 inches wide by 11 inches long. Drop immediately into 4 quarts boiling salted water, a few at a time. When water returns to a boil, cook 10 seconds and remove with slotted spoon. (If you choose to use commercial dried **lasagne,** cook the pasta until **al dente.**) Gently squeeze each noodle with hands, and rest to drain on a clean cloth towel (noodles may stick to paper towels).

2. Spread a thin coating of meat sauce over the bottom of a 12 x 14 inch **lasagne** pan, with straight sides and square corners. Add a layer of noodles, each overlapping the other very slightly. Use noodle trimmings to fill up any small openings in the layer. Spread ⅓ of the meat sauce over the noodle layer, top with ⅓ of the white sauce, and sprinkle with grated Parmesan. Continue to add layers of noodles, meat sauce, white sauce, and cheese until ingredients are used up, ending with white sauce and cheese.

3. Dot with butter and bake in a 350°F. oven until sauce is bubbly and a light crust has formed on top, about 20 to 30 minutes. Avoid overcooking, or the results will be undesirably mushy.

4. Remove from oven and let stand about 10 minutes. Cut into squares and serve.

Makes about 6 servings.

Menu suggestions. This elegant version of **lasagne** is perfect before simply prepared meat or fowl or any of the sautéed veal. Avoid second courses prepared with creamy sauces.

Stuffed Pasta Rolls (Cannelloni)

The American version of **cannelloni** usually starts with crepes as wrappers. The authentic version uses pasta dough rolled very thin and cut into large rectangles.

2 cups Basic Tomato Sauce (page 36)
2 cups White Sauce (page 36)
1 large onion, chopped
1 clove garlic, minced
¼ cup butter
1 pound boneless veal or **pork** or **ham, cubed**
1 pound chicken breasts or **thighs, boned, skinned, and chopped**
¼ teaspoon nutmeg
¼ cup chopped parsley
2 eggs
½ cup freshly grated Parmesan cheese
1 cup ricotta **cheese**
½ teaspoon salt
Basic Pasta (page 32)
4 cups mozzarella or **jack cheese, grated**

1. Prepare Basic Tomato Sauce and White Sauce, following recipe directions. Set aside.

2. In a large skillet, sauté onion and garlic in butter. Add pork, veal **or** ham, and chicken. Cover and cook over medium heat for 15 minutes, stirring occasionally. Add nutmeg and parsley. Cover and simmer an additional 15 minutes. Add a little water if mixture appears too thick. Set aside to cool.

3. Grind the cooled mixture in a food chopper or processor. Add eggs, Parmesan, **ricotta,** and salt. Mix well. Cover and refrigerate while preparing pasta.

4. Prepare pasta dough and roll out as thin as possible, then cut into 3 x 4 inch rectangles and let dry briefly. Parboil each rectangle in a small amount of salted water for 2 minutes. Drain flat on an absorbent cloth.

5. Mix Tomato Sauce and White Sauce together. Spread ½ of mixture in a 13 x 9 inch baking dish. Spoon about 3 tablespoons of the mixture down the middle of each pasta rectangle. Roll each one and place seam-side down in rows in the baking dish. Spoon remaining sauce over pasta. Sprinkle with cheese. Bake uncovered at 350°F until golden crust is formed, about 15 minutes.

Makes 8 to 10 servings.

Menu suggestions. Two **cannelloni** per serving make an ideal first course. Follow with braised meat or fowl. As a light lunch, serve **cannelloni** with a salad of asparagus or fennel in vinaigrette dressing.

Stuffed Little Hats (Cappelletti)

Northern Italians spend many hours with the whole family making these tiny tasty tidbits for Christmas and New Year's dining. They are identical to **tortellini,** except that the dough is cut into squares and shaped to resemble little pointed hats.

Start with Basic Pasta (page 32) or Spinach Pasta (page 35). Cut the rolled dough into 2-inch squares. Add a dab of filling in the center and diagonally fold one side over so that the top edge does not quite meet the bottom edge. Press to seal, then wrap around your finger and press corners together as shown in the photograph.

Cook and serve in any of the ways suggested for **tortellini.**

Stuffed Pasta Tubes (Manicotti)

A delicious recipe for stuffed **manicotti** prepared from dried tubes appears in the Ortho Book *Elegant Meals with Inexpensive Meats,* page 79.

To shape cappelletti, *cut dough into squares, place filling in center, fold into a triangle shape, and press to seal edges. Then wrap the triangle around your finger to form the pointed hat shape and press to seal. If the dough edges fail to seal, moisten with a dab of water before pressing together.*

Creamy *risotto* is one of northern Italy's greatest contributions to the world of food. In many parts of Italy it is eaten daily.

Instead of putting rice into boiling water, *risotto* is cooked by stirring the liquid into the rice, a little at a time, until the rice is creamy and tender yet firm to the bite. It is a process that can't be hurried or left unattended for a moment, but the patient care is well worthwhile. *Risotto* can be left standing only a minute or two before serving, so time its completion to coincide with your serving schedule.

With the exception of *Risotto* with Saffron Milan Style which always accompanies *Ossobuco* (page 56), *risotto* is always served as a first course. However, many American cooks will be tempted to serve *risotto* alongside meat dishes. We won't tell our Italian friends if you yield once in a while.

Basic Risotto with Parmesan Cheese (Risotto al Parmigiano)

No other versions of **risotto** can top this simple one when it is prepared with imported Parmigiano-Reggiano. Following the basic recipe are several variations, but the cooking technique stays the same no matter what you add. Create your own versions based on these ideas and ingredients you have on hand.

- **5 cups homemade Chicken Broth** or **Meat Broth (page 27)** or **regular-strength canned broth**
- **2 tablespoons olive oil**
- **3 tablespoons butter**
- **2 to 3 tablespoons finely chopped onion** or **shallots**
- **1½ cups Italian** arborio or **short-grained pearl rice**
- **½ cup freshly grated Parmesan cheese**
  Salt to taste

1. Bring stock or broth to slow simmer in a saucepan. (It will simmer throughout preparation of **risotto**.)

2. Heat the olive oil and 2 tablespoons of the butter over medium-high heat in a heavy deep frying pan or casserole. Sauté the onion or shallots until soft and lightly golden, not browned.

3. Stir in the rice and sauté until well coated with oil and butter, about 2 minutes. Add ½ cup of the simmering broth, adjusting heat if necessary so that liquid does not evaporate too fast. Keep liquid simmering and stir continually, scraping bottom and sides of the pan until liquid has evaporated.

4. Add hot broth ½ cup at a time, each time rice becomes dry, stirring continually as in Step 3. As **risotto** approaches completion, add liquid ¼ cup at a time. You may not need all the broth before the rice is done, or you may need more liquid, in which case add water. Cook until the rice is tender but firm to the bite. When properly cooked, rice should be creamy but not soupy. Total stirring time should take about 30 to 35 minutes.

5. A couple of minutes before you think the rice is done, stir in the cheese and remaining tablespoon of butter. Taste and add salt, if necessary. Serve immediately. Have a bowl of additional grated Parmesan cheese on the table for diners to add to **risotto**.

Makes 4 servings.

Risotto with Saffron Milan Style (Risotto alla Milanese)

Risotto alla Milanese is traditionally served with **Ossobuco.**

- **5 cups homemade Chicken Broth** or **Meat Broth (page 27)** or **regular-strength canned broth**
- **7 tablespoons plus 1 tablespoon butter**
- **2 to 3 tablespoons finely chopped onions** or **shallots**
- **1½ cups Italian** arborio **short-grained pearl rice**
- **½ cup dry white wine**
- **⅛ teaspoon powdered saffron** or **¼ teaspoon chopped whole saffron**
- **¼ cup freshly grated Parmesan cheese**

1. Bring stock or broth to slow simmer, as described in Step 1 of Basic **Risotto**

2. Heat 7 tablespoons of butter in a heavy, deep frying pan and sauté onions or shallots until golden. Stir in the rice and sauté until well coated.

3. Add white wine and cook, stirring, until evaporated. Begin adding broth, as described in Basic **Risotto**, Step 3. After 10 to 15 minutes of cooking, add powdered saffron **or** ½ cup broth in which you have dissolved chopped whole saffron. When that liquid evaporates, continue cooking as in Step 4 of Basic **Risotto**.

4. When **risotto** has finished cooking, stir in Parmesan, 1 tablespoon butter, and as much powdered saffron as you can afford and enjoy The **risotto** will be bright yellow according to how much saffron is added.

Risotto with Mushrooms (Risotto al Funghi)

To completed Basic **Risotto**, add ½ pound fresh mushrooms, which have been sliced and sautéed in 2 tablespoons butter in a separate pan.

For an even tastier version, soak 1 ounce of dried Italian wild mushrooms in warm water until they are limp. Drain and chop the mushrooms. Stir into the Basic **Risotto** after it has cooked about 10 minutes, then complete according to the recipe.

Risotto with Meat Sauce, Bologna Style (Risotto al Ragù)

Heat 1 cup of Northern Italian Meat Sauce, Version I **or** II (page 42) in a heavy casserole. Follow Basic **Risotto** but omit onions and reduce Parmesan cheese to ¼ cup. Add meat sauce to rice and serve.

Risotto with Tomatoes (Risotto al Pomodoro)

Proceed with Steps 1 and 2 of Basic **Risotto**. After you have stirred in the rice (Step 3), add 1 cup chopped fresh or canned Italian-style plum tomatoes and several minced fresh basil leaves **or** 1 teaspoon dried crumbled basil. Proceed as with Basic **Risotto**. After 15 minutes of cooking, add another cup of tomatoes. Just before the rice is done stir in ½ cup cream and ¼ cup minced parsley.

Creamy Risotto *with Saffron Milan Style is an elegant first course, although it is traditionally served alongside* Ossobuco *(recipe on page 56). Stir in as much powdered saffron as your budget and taste will allow.*

Risotto with Shrimp (Risotto con Gamberi)

- **1 tablespoon butter**
- **1 small onion, chopped**
- **1 pound shrimp, shelled and deveined**
- **½ cup dry white wine**
- **1 cup green peas (fresh or frozen)**
- **3 tablespoons tomato sauce**
  Salt and freshly ground black pepper to taste
  Basic Risotto

1. Heat butter over medium-high heat and sauté onion until golden. Add shrimp and wine. Stir until wine is almost evaporated. Add peas and tomato sauce. Stir until peas are done. Season with salt and pepper and set aside.

2. Begin Basic **Risotto**. After 10 minutes of cooking add ½ shrimp mixture. When the rice is done, remove pan from heat and stir in remaining shrimp mixture, one tablespoon butter, and only 1 tablespoon Parmesan cheese.

Risotto with Spring Vegetables (Risotto Primavera)

- **5 cups homemade Chicken Broth** or **Meat Broth (page 27)** or **regular-strength canned broth**
- **½ cup butter**
- **¼ cup white wine**
- **1½ cups Italian** arborio **short-grained pearl rice**
- **½ cup green peas**
- **½ cup asparagus tips**
- **½ cup diced carrots**
- **½ cup diced sweet red or yellow pepper**
- **½ cup chopped zucchini**
- **2 tablespoons diced and seeded fresh tomatoes**
- **¼ cup minced parsley**
- **½ cup freshly grated Parmesan cheese**
  Salt to taste

1. Proceed with Steps 1 and 2 of Basic **Risotto** (page 48). Stir in rice, as in Step 3.

2. Add wine and ½ portion of each vegetable. Mix rice and vegetables well to coat with butter, then begin adding broth and cook as directed in Step 3 of Basic **Risotto**.

3. When rice has cooked about 15 minutes, add the remaining vegetables and continue cooking. Just before rice is done, add tomatoes and parsley.

4. Complete as in Step 5 of Basic **Risotto**.

Potato gnocchi *dough is rolled into strips, then cut into bite-sized pieces and pressed against a fork to form the traditional shapes.*

Dumplings (Gnocchi)

Gnocchi are chewy dumplings, most often made with potato as a base, although the Roman version is prepared with *semolina* flour. They may be served in a variety of ways, topped with butter or sauce.

Potato Dumplings (Gnocchi di Patate)

Gnocchi may be served in **Pesto** Sauce (page 36), Basic Tomato Sauce (page 36), Northern Italian Meat Sauce, Cream, Butter, and Cheese Sauce (page 37), or any of your own favorites.

> **2 pounds Idaho baking potatoes (the older the better), unpeeled**
> **About 1½ cups flour**
> **1 teaspoon salt**
> **1 egg, slightly beaten (optional)**

1. Cook potatoes whole in boiling salted water until tender. Drain and peel, then purée in a food processor, potato ricer, or put through a medium sieve. Place purée in a large bowl.

2. Add 1 cup of the flour, the salt, and the egg. Knead with fingers until smooth, adding more flour a little at a time until dough is no longer sticky.

3. Shape into long rolls about ¾ inch thick, then cut into lengths about 1¼ inches long. With your fingers, press each piece against the back of a fork so that side will have the impression of the tines and the other will have a dent in the middle made by your finger; **or** roll each piece against the work surface with your finger to form a bow shape. (Gnocchi machines are available to automate the shaping.) Rest completed **gnocchi** on a lightly dusted board.

4. Cook immediately after shaping all the dough. Drop about ⅓ at a time into 4 quarts boiling salted water. After they rise to the surface, continue to cook about 10 to 15 seconds, then remove with slotted spoon to a heated bowl and toss in a little melted butter or some of the heated sauce you plan to serve them in. Cover the container with foil to keep warm while you cook the rest of the **gnocchi**.

5. To serve, pour selected sauce over **gnocchi**, add about ⅔ cup grated Parmesan or **romano** cheese, and mix well. Pass additional grated cheese at the table.

Makes 6 servings.

Menu suggestions. The sauce selected will determine what is compatible with the **gnocchi** first course. Choose an **antipasto** and a second course that will not conflict with the sauce.

Baked Semolina Cakes, Roman Style (Gnocchi alla Romana)

For busy cooks here's a pasta course you can prepare a day or two ahead. Refrigerate tightly covered, then bake at the last minute.

> **4 cups milk**
> **1½ teaspoons salt**
> **Freshly ground nutmeg and black pepper**
> **1½ cups** semolina
> **1 cup freshly grated Parmesan cheese**
> **2 eggs, slightly beaten**
> **⅓ cup melted butter**
> **¼ cup minced fresh parsley**
> **1 tablespoon crumbled dried sage leaves**

1. Combine milk, salt, and a pinch of nutmeg and pepper in a saucepan. Bring milk just to the point of boiling. Reduce heat and gradually pour in **semolina** in a thin stream, stirring constantly with a wooden spoon or beating with a wire wisk. Continue cooking and stirring until **semolina** is thick enough for the spoon to stand upright, about 15 minutes. Remove from heat.

2. Stir ¾ cup Parmesan cheese, egg yolks, and 2 tablespoons butter into the **semolina**, blending well.

3. Butter a large shallow baking sheet. Using a metal spatula dipped in cold water from time to time, spread the thick mixture into a layer about ¼ inch thick. Refrigerate for about 1 hour, or until **semolina** is firm.

4. With a 1½ inch biscuit cutter occasionally dipped in cold water cut **semolina** into rounds. Place in a buttered 9-inch (23 cm) baking dish in slightly overlaping rows to form a single layer. Dribble with melted butter and sprinkle with remaining Parmesan. Top with minced parsley and sage. Bake at 400° F (200° C) until golden and crusty, about 15 minutes. If necessary run the dish under a preheated hot broiler for about 30 seconds to lightly brown.

Makes 4 to 6 servings.

Roman-style gnocchi *is made by cutting rounds of cooked semolina mixture and placing them in a baking pan to simulate overlapping shingles. Top the* gnocchi *with cheese, herbs, and butter before baking.*

Use the palms of your hands to roll spinach and ricotta mixture into balls for Gnocchi Verde.

Spinach Dumplings (Gnocchi Verde)

Green **gnocchi** can be prepared several hours ahead of time, or frozen for later use, then dropped into boiling water for cooking just before serving. Sauce the same as Potato Dumplings or use the one that follows.

1 pound fresh spinach, chopped, or 10-ounce package frozen chopped spinach, thawed completely	**2 eggs, beaten**
	¼ cup freshly grated Parmesan cheese
	¼ cup finely chopped green onion
1½ cups ricotta **cheese**	**½ teaspoon salt**
1 cup fine dry bread crumbs	**1 teaspoon nutmeg Flour**

Sauce

2 tablespoons butter	**½ teaspoon tarragon**
3 tablespoons flour	**Pinch of nutmeg**
2½ cups milk	**Salt and freshly ground black pepper to taste**
½ cup homemade Chicken Broth (page 27) or regular-strength canned broth	**½ to ¾ cup freshly grated Parmesan cheese**

Topping

3 tablespoons fine white breadcrumbs

2 tablespoons freshly grated Parmesan cheese

1. If you are using fresh spinach, wilt the leaves for about 30 seconds in a kettle of boiling salted water. Drain spinach well by putting it in a sieve or colander and pressing with a wooden spoon. When it's drained, chop finely.

2. In a mixing bowl combine spinach, **ricotta** cheese, bread crumbs, eggs, Parmesan cheese, onion, and seasonings. Blend well and refrigerate for about 2 hours.

3. When chilled, form the **gnocchi** by rolling about 1 teaspoon of the mixture between the palms of your hands into small, walnut-sized balls. Roll lightly in flour. Arrange on a tray lined with waxed paper. Refrigerate until cooking time.

4. To prepare sauce, melt butter in a saucepan. When it begins to froth, add the flour and stir frequently over medium heat. Meanwhile, bring the milk and stock to a simmer. After the flour and butter mixture has cooked for 4 or 5 minutes, remove pan from heat. When cooled slightly, add the simmering liquid all at once and blend with a wire whisk until smooth.

5. Return the saucepan to medium heat and stir until the sauce coats a spoon lightly and no flour taste remains. Add the seasonings. Taste carefully and simmer 2 to 3 minutes. Add the cheese and blend until fully incorporated.

6. In a large kettle, bring several quarts of salted water to a simmer. Drop in the **gnocchi** a few at a time, depending upon the size of the kettle, and regulate the heat so the water remains at a simmer. **Gnocchi** are done when they pop up to the surface.

7. Remove the cooked dumplings to a buttered baking dish, using a slotted spoon for ease in handling. Continue until all the **gnocchi** have been cooked.

8. Fold the sauce into the **gnocchi** in the baking dish. Sprinkle on the cheese and breadcrumbs and place under a hot broiler for 2 or 3 minutes to melt the cheese and brown the breadcrumbs. Serve immediately.

Makes 4 servings.

Menu suggestions. This dish can precede any roasted, grilled, or sautéed meat or fowl.

Pour polenta *in a steady stream into boiling salted water, stirring constantly. Continue to stir frequently until mixture reaches desired thickness. For traditionally thick* polenta *a spoon should stand straight up before the mixture is poured out onto a serving platter or wooden board. Smooth the surface with a water-dampened spoon.*

Polenta

Long ago, in the regions of northern Italy around Venice and Florence where *polenta* was (and still is) eaten daily, the coarse cornmeal was cooked over the fireplace in an unlined copper kettle. Today *polenta* is cooked on top of the stove in a tapered copper pan, and a regular saucepan can be used with almost equal success.

Polenta is usually considered ready to eat when it is so thick that a spoon can stand upright in it. Then the *polenta* is poured onto a plate or wooden surface to set for a few minutes before serving, or to cool before it is sliced for further cooking. Southern Italian cooks, however, prefer a thinner version (*polentina*) cooked to the texture of cream of wheat, poured hot into bowls, and topped with cheese and butter or a favorite simmered sauce, such as one of the meat sauces.

There are several ways to vary *polenta*, but they all begin with the same basic recipe.

Basic Polenta

- **6 cups water** or **up to 10 cups water for thinner** polentina
- **1 tablespoon salt**
- **2 cups** polenta **or coarse-grained cornmeal**

1. In a copper **polenta** pan or heavy saucepan, bring water to boil, add salt, and reduce heat so water is just simmering. Gradually add **polenta** in a steady stream, stirring constantly with a long-handled wooden spoon.

2. Continue to stir quite frequently until **polenta** is thickened to your preference. Thick, sliceable **polenta** should come away from the sides of the pot and be able to support a spoon. Thin **polentina** should be the texture of thick cream of wheat.

3. Pour thin **polentina** into bowls ready to serve. Pour thick **polenta** directly onto wooden board or platter, or pour into a buttered shallow bowl and let stand a few minutes before turning out onto a serving platter. **Polenta** can be served as is to accompany a second course, or as a bed for grilled quail or other birds, rabbit stew, or sausages. As a first course, **polenta** may be topped with grated cheese. To serve with sauce, make indentations in the top with a spoon and pour sauce into these. Or the mixture can be allowed to cool completely, sliced, and cooked as suggested in the variations that follow. Traditionally, **polenta** is cut with a tautly held string, but it's easier with a knife.
Makes 4 to 6 servings.

Polenta Pie (Polenta Pasticciata)

As an alternative to **lasagne**, cut cold **polenta** into ¼-inch-thick slices and make a layer of the slices in a buttered **lasagne** pan. Top with layers of Italian White Sauce (page 36) and 2 cups Norma's Meat Sauce (page 43) **or** Northern Italian Meat Sauce (page 42) and 1 cup freshly grated Parmesan cheese. Continue layering until you have used up all ingredients. Dot the final sprinkling of Parmesan with butter and bake at 450°F until the top is crusty, about 15 minutes.

Polenta with Cheese (Polenta al Formaggio)

Cook **polenta** according to basic recipe (this page). Just as **polenta** is thickened to your preference, stir in about ⅓ cup grated Parmesan or **Romano** cheese **or** shredded **fontina or** other melting cheese, and ½ cup butter cut into small pieces. Stir until cheese and butter are melted, pour out, and serve immediately as a first course.

Fried Polenta (Polenta Fritta)

Cut cold **polenta** into slices, rounds, or wedges and fry in hot vegetable oil or butter about ¾ inch deep in a skillet over high heat. Turn to cook all sides until a transparent crust forms, but not until browned. Drain on paper towels and serve with roasted or grilled meats, fish, or fowl **or** as part of a mixed fry along with Fried Vegetables (page 69) and assorted fried meats. The Venetians serve white or yellow cornmeal fried **polenta** with their famous Venetian Liver (page 58).

Although it is most definitely **not** authentic, try **polenta** fried in butter, sprinkled with powdered sugar, and drizzled with honey or hot maple syrup for a breakfast treat **or** spread with jam for afternoon tea.

Second Courses (Secondi Piatti)

In comparison to the often gloriously rich first courses, Italian second courses are quite simple, a welcome contrast. Meat, fowl, and fish may be sautéed, fried, roasted, broiled, or boiled. The meat may be seasoned simply, or served with a sauce.

Our recipes begin with veal, the most popular second course. Following recipes for meats, poultry, and fish are recipes for *frittati* (open-faced Italian omelets) and Spinach and Cheese Pie. Both can be adapted as second courses for vegetarians.

Although game is an important part of Italian dining, it's often difficult to find in the U.S. However, you will find a recipe for Rabbit Stew (page 59), which can be prepared with commercially raised rabbits, and recipes for Braised Squab (page 60) and Charcoal-Grilled Quail (page 61).

Veal Scallops with Lemon (recipe on the next page) is prepared in a matter of minutes. The tangy scallops are great with Broccoli sauteed with Garlic (page 67.)

Sautéed Veal Scallops (Scaloppine di Vitello)

Scaloppine, probably the most popular second course in Italian restaurants, is prepared in almost as many variations as there are chefs.

Meat Preparation. Ask your butcher to cut veal about ¼ inch thick from top round, cutting across the grain to produce meat without muscle separations (these cause the meat to shrivel when cooked). Ask your butcher to pound the meat flat, or place the thinly sliced veal between two sheets of waxed paper and pound with wooden or metal mallet as flat and thin as possible (about ⅛ inch thick) without breaking meat.

Dredge or dip scallops into flour at the last minute to avoid a damp coating that won't brown correctly. Shake off excess flour before adding to the hot oil.

Sautéeing Veal. Be sure oil or butter is quite hot, to cook veal quickly and maintain tenderness. Sauté veal over medium-high heat until lightly browned on one side, then turn and brown second side. The total cooking time should take only about 1 minute. Do not overcook, or the meat will be tough. Remove to warm plate and complete sauce in the pan according to recipes that follow.

For variety or economy, prepare any of the following veal sauté recipes with pounded boneless chicken or turkey breast, or a tender cut of beef prepared as above.

The following variations make 4 servings each.

Pound veal with a heavy mallet to flatten and tenderize. Dust with flour before quickly sautéeing in butter and olive oil.

Veal Scallops with Lemon (Picatta di Vitello)

1 pound thinly sliced veal scaloppine, **pounded according to directions on page 53**
Flour
3 tablespoons oil
3 tablespoons butter
2 tablespoons freshly squeezed lemon juice
2 tablespoons minced parsley
Salt and freshly ground black pepper to taste
Lemon slices and minced parsley for garnish

1. Dredge **scaloppine** in flour and sauté as directed above. Remove to warm platter.

2. Over very low heat, add lemon juice and parsley to the skillet and scrape all cooking residue from sides and bottom. Add 2 tablespoons butter and stir until butter melts. Pour sauce over **scaloppine**, add salt and pepper. Garnish and serve immediately.

Menu suggestions. Fettuccine with Butter, Cream, and Cheese Sauce (page 37), or Pasta with Northern Italian Meat Sauce (page 42), make a good first course. Accompany the **scaloppine** with Broccoli Sautéed with Garlic (page 67).

Veal Scallops, Milan Style (Scaloppine alla Milanese)

1 egg, beaten
Salt and freshly ground black pepper to taste
1 pound thinly sliced veal scaloppine, pounded according to directions
1 cup dry, unseasoned bread crumbs
3 tablespoons butter
3 tablespoons olive oil
Lemon slices and chopped parsley for garnish

1. Season beaten egg with salt and pepper, and immerse veal in this mixture for several minutes, until evenly coated. Remove veal and dip into breadcrumbs just before sautéeing, pressing with fingers to make sure crumbs adhere.

2. Sauté **scaloppine** in hot butter and oil as directed on page 53, and serve immediately with pan drippings. Garnish with lemon slices and chopped parsley.

Menu suggestions. Precede with **Risotto** Milan Style (page 48), and accompany with Peas Sautéed with **Prosciutto** (page 67).

Veal Scallops with Tomato Sauce (Scaloppine alla Pizzaiola)

1 pound thinly sliced veal, pounded according to directions on page 53
Flour
Salt and freshly ground black pepper to taste
3 tablespoons olive oil
½ cup dry white wine
1 tablespoon tomato paste
1 tablespoon butter
1 teaspoon dried oregano, crumbled
Parsley, coarsely chopped, for garnish

1. Dredge **scaloppine** in flour and brown in hot oil, as directed on page 53. Transfer to warmed platter and add salt and pepper.

2. Pour off all but about 1 tablespoon of the oil. Add wine, and scrape drippings from bottom and sides of pan. Stir in tomato paste, butter, and oregano, and cook until slightly thickened. Return scallops to pan and turn once to coat both sides with tomato sauce. Arrange on serving platter and pour sauce over top. Garnish with parsley.

Menu suggestions. Begin meal with any soup or pasta that doesn't contain tomato. No vegetable accompaniment is necessary, but any Fried Vegetable (page 69) would be delicious.

Veal Scallops with Prosciutto and Sage (Saltimbocca alla Romana)

1 pound thinly sliced veal, pounded according to directions on page 53
½ pound prosciutto, thinly sliced
Whole sage leaves, fresh or dried
2 tablespoons butter
¼ cup olive oil
Salt and freshly ground black pepper to taste
1 cup dry white wine

1. Top each veal scallop with one or two sage leaves and a slice of **prosciutto**. Secure with a toothpick.

2. Brown in hot butter and oil, add salt and pepper and white wine, reduce heat and simmer about 5 minutes. Transfer veal to warmed platter, remove toothpicks.

3. Turn up heat and boil until pan juices are reduced by ½. Pour over meat and serve immediately.

Menu suggestions. Start with a **risotto** or pasta in broth. As an accompaniment to the veal, consider Asparagus Parmesan (page 66).

Roasted Veal (Arrosto di Vitello)

Flavorful pan-roasted veal is Italian peasant cookery at its best. Tradition dictates serving the roast already sliced before bringing to the table, a carryover from Roman days when guests weren't to be trusted with knives.

- **1¹/₂ to 2 pounds flat boned veal roast, preferably top round**
- **¹/₂ teaspoon crushed peppercorns**
- **2 tablespoons minced garlic**
- **1 teaspoon chopped fresh rosemary or crumbled dried**
- **5 to 6 whole sage leaves, torn**
- **3 tablespoons butter**
- **2 tablespoons vegetable oil**
- **1 teaspoon salt to taste**
- **¹/₂ cup dry white wine**
- **3 to 4 tablespoons chopped parsley for garnish**

1. Spread roast with peppercorns, garlic, rosemary, and sage. Roll and tie securely. (If using a round piece of roast, gash in several places and insert seasonings.)

2. Heat butter and oil over medium-high heat in a Dutch oven or heavy casserole and brown meat on all sides, about 15 minutes. Add salt and wine. When wine comes to a boil, reduce heat to simmer and cover. Turn roast occasionally and cook until fork tender, about 1¹/₂ to 2 hours. Add a little water if necessary to maintain some liquid during cooking.

3. Remove roast from pan, slice, and arrange on preheated platter. Pour pan drippings over meat slices. Gravy may be thickened with cornstarch, if desired. Garnish down the center with chopped parsley.

Makes about 6 servings.

Stuffed variations. Before rolling and tying, a flat roast may be spread with Herb-Seasoned Breadcrumbs (page 71) combined with ground meat **or** your own favorite stuffing mixture.

Menu suggestions. Veal roast is one of those dishes that can follow any first course. It's best served with a green vegetable, such as broccoli or zucchini. Grilled tomatoes topped with Parmesan cheese are a nice accent on the plate.

Skewered Veal Birds (Spiedini alla Uccelletto)

- **2 pounds veal cut from the leg, cut into 1¹/₂-inch cubes**
- **2 cups Herb-Seasoned Breadcrumbs (page 71)**
- **1 teaspoon powdered sage**
- **2 eggs, beaten**
- **¹/₂ teaspoon salt Freshly ground black pepper to taste**
- **4 tablespoons vegetable oil**
- **2 cups Basic Tomato Sauce (page 36)**

1. Divide meat into 6 to 8 equal portions and thread onto small wooden skewers. Number of skewers needed will depend upon the size of the pieces of meat and the length of the skewers.

2. In a flat dish, combine breadcrumbs and sage, blending together thoroughly.

3. In another bowl combine eggs with salt and pepper.

4. Dip meat skewers into beaten eggs, then roll in seasoned breadcrumbs. Set aside to dry for about 15 minutes.

5. Heat oil in a large skillet over medium heat. Slowly brown meat on all sides. Transfer to a flat, covered baking dish. Cover with Basic Tomato Sauce, and bake at 350°F for 1 hour. Check occasionally and add more sauce if necessary. Uncover and bake an additional 30 minutes.

Makes 6 to 8 servings.

Menu suggestions. Serve with spaghetti or other homemade noodles **or** on a bed of **polenta**. If you want a vegetable accompaniment, try crunchy Braised Fennel or Broccoli Sautéed with Garlic (page 67).

Variation. Equal parts of veal, pork, and beef cubes can be used instead of all veal.

Stuffed Rigatoni with Veal Rolls (Rigatoni Ripieni con Involtini di Vitello)

A creamy filling, rich with cheese, is used to stuff the large tubular **rigatoni**. Combined with delicately flavored veal rolls and baked in a zesty tomato sauce, this is a favorite make-ahead casserole.

- **¹/₂ pound rigatoni**
- **4 slices bacon**
- **8 veal scallops, pounded thin**
- **3 tablespoons chopped pine nuts**
- **3 tablespoons minced parsley**
- **2 tablespoons olive oil**

Sauce
- **2 cloves garlic, crushed**
- **2 tablespoons olive oil**
- **2 1-pound cans Italian-style plum tomatoes**
- **2 tablespoons tomato paste**
- **2 tablespoons sugar**
- **1 teaspoon salt Freshly ground black pepper, to taste**
- **¹/₂ teaspoon basil**
- **¹/₂ teaspoon marjoram**

Filling
- **1¹/₂ pounds ricotta cheese**
- **³/₄ cup shredded mozzarella cheese**
- **1 teaspoon salt Freshly ground black pepper to taste**

Topping
- **¹/₄ cup freshly grated Parmesan cheese**

1. Cook **rigatoni** in boiling, salted water until al **dente**, as described on page 36. Drain, rinse with cold water, and set aside to cool.

2. Fry bacon, drain until partially cooled, and reserve drippings. Cut slices in half. Lay a piece of bacon on each slice of veal. Divide pine nuts and parsley equally between the 8 slices. Roll up veal tightly and secure with toothpicks.

3. Sauté veal rolls in reserved bacon drippings and 2 tablespoons olive oil until golden brown on all sides. Cover and simmer until tender, 15 to 20 minutes. Drain, remove toothpicks, and cut each roll into 3 pieces.

4. To make sauce, sauté garlic in 2 tablespoons olive oil. Add tomatoes and remaining sauce ingredients and simmer for 30 minutes.

5. While sauce is simmering, combine filling ingredients. Using a small spoon, stuff each **rigatoni** shell.

6. Arrange stuffed **rigatoni** and veal rolls in a 2-quart baking dish. Spoon tomato sauce over rolls and sprinkle with Parmesan cheese topping.

7. Bake, uncovered, in a 350°F oven for 45 minutes, or until heated through.

Makes 6 servings.

Veal cutlets as prepared in Milan.

Luciano's Veal Shanks with Green Peas (Ossobuco)

Ossobuco is the Italian word for "hollow bones." In reality, the bones of veal shanks are rich in marrow that is spooned out and eaten along with meat made tender by slow cooking. Select meatier hind shanks, and have the butcher remove each end of the shank and saw the remainder into 2-inch pieces (or longer), leaving skin intact. This version was shared by Luciano Parolari of the Villa d'Este Hotel on Lake Como, north of Milan, where the dish originated. Like many Italian dishes **Ossobucco** is finished off with **Gremolada**.

Salt and freshly ground black pepper
8 veal shanks
Flour
2 tablespoons butter
2 tablespoons vegetable oil
1 carrot, finely chopped
1 onion, finely chopped
1 celery stalk, finely chopped
¼ teaspoon sage
¼ teaspoon rosemary

1 bay leaf
1 cup dry white wine
2 to 3 tablespoons tomato sauce or canned Italian-style plum tomatoes, chopped
2 cups homemade Beef Broth or Chicken Broth (page 27) or regular-strength canned broth
2 cups cooked green peas, fresh or frozen

Gremolada
3 tablespoons chopped parsley

1 clove garlic, crushed
1 lemon rind, grated

1. Salt and pepper the veal shanks, roll in flour, and brown meat in butter and oil over medium-high heat.

2. Remove veal and set aside. Add vegetables and herbs to the butter and oil and sauté the vegetables briefly. Add wine and cook rapidly to reduce the liquid.

3. Return meat to pan (keep shanks upright to prevent marrow from escaping). Add tomato sauce and stock, cover, and cook gently over low heat until tender. Usual cooking time is about 1½ hours, but this varies according to the quality of the meat.

4. When the meat is tender, stir in peas. Remove bay leaf. Combine ingredients for **Gremolada**, add, simmer for about 10 minutes before serving.

Makes 8 servings.

Variation. Can be prepared with beef knuckles; these require longer cooking.

Veal Cutlet Milan Style (Cotolette alla Milanese)

For a change of pace, substitute slices of chicken or turkey breast, or a tender cut of beef for the veal.

6 ¼-inch thick veal scallops, cut from the leg, pounded according to directions on page 53
1 cup milk
Flour seasoned with salt and freshly ground black pepper to taste
2 eggs, well beaten
Herb-seasoned Breadcrumbs (page 71)
Vegetable oil and butter
Lemon slices and chopped parsley for garnish

1. Place veal scallops in a shallow platter and cover with milk; allow to stand for about an hour. Drain and dry well.

2. Dip veal first into flour, then into beaten eggs, and finally cover each slice with breadcrumbs, pressing with fingers to make sure crumbs adhere evenly.

3. In a wide skillet, heat ¼-inch-deep layer of ½ butter and ½ oil. When hot, sauté meat for about 5 minutes on each side or until golden brown and crisp.

4. Transfer to heated platter, garnish with slices of lemon and parsley. Serve immediately.

Makes 6 servings.

Note. In summer, this dish is marvelous served cold; good picnic fare anytime.

Stuffed Beef Roll in Tomato Sauce (Bracciola Involtino di Manzo)

Not a dish to be prepared at the last minute, this tasty stuffed beef roll can be made ahead of time and kept in the refrigerator until ready to roast.

1 2-pound slice of beef top round steak, cut about 1-inch thick
1 cup Herb-Seasoned Breadcrumbs (page 71)
Olive oil
3 to 4 ounces Italian dry salami, thinly sliced
3 to 4 ounces provolone, thinly sliced
1 hard-cooked egg, chopped
3 tablespoons vegetable oil
1 clove garlic, minced
½ cup chopped onion
2 cups quartered canned Italian-style plum tomatoes
1 bay leaf
½ teaspoon salt
½ teaspoon oregano
1 tablespoon tomato paste
½ cup dry red wine

1. Butterfly steak by slicing almost in half horizontally. Open out flat on cutting board and pound to about ¼-inch thickness, using a meat mallet.

2. Brush surface with olive oil and spread with Herb-Seasoned Breadcrumbs; spread salami, **provolone**, and hard-cooked egg evenly over crumbs. Roll as for a jellyroll. Tie with string in 3 or 4 places.

3. Heat oil in a heavy, oven-proof skillet or Dutch oven. Brown well on all sides. Remove roll and set aside.

4. Add garlic and onion to skillet; cook over medium heat until soft and golden. Stir in tomatoes, bay leaf, salt, oregano, and tomato paste. Bring to a boil, stirring.

5. Return beef roll to skillet; cover and bake at 350°F for 2 hours or until meat is fork tender. Remove cover, add wine, and bake for 20 minutes or until sauce is thickened.

6. Transfer roll to a warm platter; let sit for 30 minutes to firm up, remove strings, then carve into 1-inch slices. Serve steak with additional sauce.

Menu suggestions. Serve with pasta or homemade noodles. Accompany with a crisp green salad or any vegetable that does not use tomatoes in its preparation.

Slowly simmered veal shanks or Ossobuco *are served atop saffron-rich* Risotto *Milan Style (page 48). Be sure to spoon out the marrow from the bones for a taste treat.*

Cold Stuffed Beef Roll (Bisteca Fredda Imbottita)

Prepare this tasty stuffed roll a day or two ahead. It is easy to slice and arrange on a platter just before serving.

1½ pound slice beef steak, preferably top round, with no holes or connecting tissue
¼ pound mortadella, sliced ⅛ inch thick
¼ cup chopped onion
2 tablespoons olive oil
1 clove garlic, minced
2 tablespoons chopped parsley
1 package frozen chopped spinach, cooked and well drained
½ cup ricotta cheese
¼ cup freshly grated Parmesan cheese
¼ cup dry bread crumbs
1 egg, beaten
½ teaspoon nutmeg
Salt and freshly ground black pepper to taste
2 tablespoons oil or butter
½ cup dry white wine
½ cup water or beef broth

1. Lay beef on flat surface and pound to ¼-inch thickness. Layer **mortadella** slices on top.

2. Sauté onion in oil over medium heat until transparent. Add garlic and parsley. Cook for a few minutes and remove from heat. Combine with spinach, **ricotta** and Parmesan cheeses, bread-crumbs, egg, nutmeg, and salt and pepper to taste.

3. Spread spinach mixture in an even layer over **morta-della**. Roll up meat jellyroll fashion and tie securely with strings. Wrap with a double layer of cheesecloth, knot-ting each end and leaving them long enough to serve as handles for removing meat later.

4. Brown the meat roll on all sides over high heat in oil or butter. Add wine and let it re-duce slightly. Sprinkle meat with salt and pepper and add water or beef broth. cover, lower heat, and cook slowly for about 2 hours, adding more water or broth if necessary.

5. Remove from heat and let cool in cooking liquid. Re-move roll to a platter, cover, and refrigerate several hours, preferably overnight, before removing cheesecloth and strings.

6. Slice into thin slices and arrange attractively on a serving platter.

Makes about 6 servings.

Steak Florentine (Bisteca alla Fiorentina)

This is Italian cookery at its simplest, and there's nothing better when good meat is selected. Although in America the word Florentine often means that the dish contains spinach, here it simply means the way steak is prepared in Florence.

2 steaks (rib or sirloin), about 2 inches thick
Black peppercorns, crushed
Salt
Olive Oil
Juice of 1 lemon

1. Build fire in grill with fra-grant wood or charcoal. Reduce to glowing embers and adjust grill to 3 to 4 inches from heat.

2. Have steaks at room tem-perature, if possible. Rub pepper into both sides of steaks. Grill one side for 3 minutes for rare or 5 minutes for medium rare, turn and salt cooked side. Grill sec-ond side in same way, turn and salt. Never cook a Steak Florentine to well done.

3. Place on heated serving platter, drizzle with a few drops of olive oil and a squeeze of lemon juice.

Makes 4 servings.

Italian Hamburger Variations

Budget-conscious hosts can turn the American hamburger into an Italian treat with one of the following variations.

Top burger patty with chopped marinated artichoke hearts, cover with sliced **fontina** cheese, and cook briefly under the broiler.

Spoon **Pesto** Sauce (page 36) over charcoal-grilled ham-burger.

Serve the grilled hamburger on slices of tomato-flavored **focaccia** bread or grilled garlic bread.

Add ¼ pound minced **prosciutto** and 2 egg yolks to 1 pound ground beef. Grill, then drizzle with olive oil.

Top almost-cooked patties with flattened canned Italian-style plum tomatoes. Sprinkle with oregano and cover with slice of **mozzarella** cheese. Top with an anchovy filet and place in hot oven or under broiler until cheese melts.

Top grilled patties with **Gorgonzola** cheese and put briefly under broiler to melt cheese. Serve on onion roll.

Boned leg of lamb slowly pan roasted according to the recipe on page 58 produces a succulent dish. Baked Stuffed Tomatoes (page 68) may precede the lamb or be served as a side dish.

Pan-Roasted Spring Lamb (Abbacchio)

In Italy, suckling lamb (**abbacchio**) is a welcome early spring delicacy. In America, however, the youngest butchered spring lamb is somewhat older. Pan roasting produces a tender, succulent dish just the same.

- **2 to 2½-pound leg of spring lamb**
- **3 tablespoons butter**
- **3 tablespoons vegetable oil**
- **1 teaspoon minced garlic**
- **1 teaspoon crumbled dried rosemary**
- **1 teaspoon crumbled dried sage**
- **Salt and freshly ground black pepper to taste**
- **¾ cup dry white wine**

1. Brown lamb on all sides in butter and oil over medium-high heat in a heavy pan. Add garlic, rosemary, sage, salt, pepper, and wine. Increase heat until wine comes to boil.

2. Reduce heat and cover pan. Simmer until lamb is very tender when pierced with a fork, from 1 to 2 hours.

Add a little water if pan becomes dry while cooking, and turn lamb occasionally.

3. Place lamb on preheated serving platter. Spoon off all but 1 tablespoon of the cooking fat. Add 2 tablespoons water or wine and increase heat, scraping residue from bottom and sides of the pan. Pour over lamb.

Makes 4 servings.

Menu suggestions. Lamb is good after any pasta except those prepared with fish. Stuffed Artichokes (page 65) may be served with lamb, either as an **antipasto** or as a stand-in for the first course. Accompany the lamb with one of the early spring vegetables such as asparagus or tiny green peas. Or serve with Stuffed Tomatoes.

Liver Venetian Style (Fegato alla Veneziana)

To achieve the sweet flavor of this famed delicacy of Venice, start with very young, tender calf liver sliced no more than ¼ inch thick, and cook it quickly. The onions, on the other hand, should be cooked slowly and separately to bring out their flavor.

- **1½ pounds calf liver, thinly sliced**
- **3 tablespoons olive oil**
- **3 cups thinly sliced yellow onions**
- **Salt and freshly ground black pepper to taste**

1. Trim any gristle from the liver. Cut liver into bite-sized strips.

2. Heat oil over medium heat in a 12-inch skillet and cook onions slowly 15 to 20 minutes, or until limp and golden. Do not let them burn or stick to pan.

3. Remove onions with a slotted spoon and reserve, leaving any excess oil in pan.

4. Turn heat to high. When oil is very hot, toss in the sliced liver and cook about 1 minute, or until just browned. Turn strips and add salt, pepper, and onions. Turn the entire mixture again, cooking no longer than 1 minute more, and transfer to a warm serving dish. Serve immediately.

Makes 4 servings.

Variation. Substitute Herb-Seasoned Breadcrumbs (page 71) for the flour coating. Proceed in the same manner.

Sausage with Red Wine (Salsicce al Vino Rosso)

Italian sausage prepared in this manner and served in crusty warm rolls is a popular treat.

- **2½ pounds Italian sausage, sweet or hot or a combination of both**
- **2 cups cold water, approximately**
- **⅓ cup dry red wine**
- **2 tablespoons olive oil**
- **3 large onions, sliced**
- **3 large bell peppers, seeded and sliced**
- **6 to 8 crusty French or Italian rolls, split and warmed**

1. Prick casings of sausages with a fork and place in a cold skillet. Add cold water to cover and boil briskly for 3 minutes. Lower heat to simmer and cook for 20 minutes or until most of the water evaporates. Drain any remaining liquid and allow sausages to brown on all sides. Gradually add wine, cover, and simmer for an additional 5 minutes.

2. In another skillet, combine olive oil, onions, and peppers. Cook and stir over low heat until vegetables are just tender but still crisp. Salt and pepper to taste.

3. Place hot sausages in warm rolls and fill with cooked pepper and onion mixture. Serve immediately.

Makes 6 to 8 servings.

Sausages with Lentils (Salsicce con Lenticchie)

- **1 pound mild Italian sausage**
- **2 tablespoons olive oil**
- **½ cup finely minced celery**
- **½ cup finely minced carrots**
- **1 medium onion, chopped**
- **1 large clove garlic, minced**
- **1 tablespoon minced parsley**
- **2 cups dried lentils, washed and picked over**
- **4 cups homemade Beef Stock (page 27) or regular-strength canned broth**
- **1 cup coarsely chopped fresh or canned Italian-style plum tomatoes**
- **2 teaspoons salt**
- **½ teaspoon pepper**
- **1 bay leaf**
- **¼ cup rice**
- **¼ cup dry white wine (optional)**

1. Pierce sausage casings and place in cold skillet. Cover with boiling water, cover, and simmer for 10 minutes. Reserve 2 tablespoons of the liquid and discard the rest. Cut sausages into 1-inch pieces and return to skillet. Brown evenly on all sides, then set aside.

2. In large Dutch oven, combine olive oil, celery, carrots, onion, garlic, and parsley. Cook until vegetables are tender, about 5 minutes. Add lentils, beef broth, tomatoes, salt, pepper, and bay leaf. Bring to a boil, reduce heat, cover, and simmer slowly until lentils are tender, about 2 hours, stirring occasionally.

3. Add rice to lentil mixture, cover, and cook for another 30 minutes. Check occasionally and add more beef broth if mixture gets too thick. Add sausage pieces and white wine and cook for an additional 10 minutes. Remove bay leaf before serving.

Makes 8 servings.

Wild mushrooms are featured in the market-places of Italy. In America they're available dried.

Stewed Rabbit (Coniglio in Umido)

Italian cuisine offers rabbit, both wild and domestic, prepared in a variety of ways. This simple version uses domestic rabbits, either fresh or frozen. If you have access to fresh domestic rabbits, rinse several times in cold water, then pat dry with paper towels. Frozen rabbits should be thawed overnight in the refrigerator.

- **2 fresh or frozen rabbits, whole or cut up** **Marinade (recipe folows)**
- **4 cloves garlic, pressed or finely minced**
- **1 teaspoon crumbled dried rosemary**
- **1 teaspoon freshly ground black pepper**
- **2/3 cup vegetable oil**
- **2 teaspoons Worcester- shire sauce**
- **3 large yellow onions, chopped,** or **10 green onions, including tops, chopped**

- **2 chicken or beef bouillon cubes**
- **1 1/2 cups hot water**
- **2 6-ounce cans tomato paste**
- **1 lemon** or **1 lime** or **5 tablespoons lemon juice**
- **20 black olives**
- **1 cup red wine**
- **2 large** or **4 small zucchini, cut into 1/2-inch slices**
- **2 stalks celery, finely chopped**

Marinade

- **1/4 cup vinegar**
- **1 clove garlic, pressed or minced**

- **1 teaspoon salt**
- **1 teabag**
- **2 cups hot water**

1. Place rabbits in a large pot with marinade and allow to soak for 10 hours, or over-night. (Frozen rabbits may be boiled for 10 minutes in the marinade with enough water added to cover rab-bits, then allowed to soak in the marinade overnight.) Drain well.

2. Rub garlic, rosemary, and black pepper over the out-side and interior cavities of the drained rabbits. Brown in oil in 12-inch skillet over me-dium-high heat until well browned on all sides, approx-imately 15 to 20 minutes.

3. Sprinkle Worcestershire sauce over meat and add chopped onions to the pan.

4. Dissolve bouillon cubes in hot water. Add tomato paste and stir to mix thor-oughly; pour over meat.

5. Squeeze lemon or lime juice over meat and reduce heat to medium-low. Add olives and wine, then stir in zucchini and celery, turning all ingredients gently to mix well. Reduce heat to lowest possible temperature. Cover pan and simmer 2 hours or until tender, stirring and bast-ing occasionally. Add water, if necessary, to avoid drying the meat.

Rabbit is done when a skewer or fork passes through the flesh easily.

Makes 4 to 6 servings.

Note. Rabbit may be stewed longer or cooked ahead and reheated slowly, add-ing a little water to prevent drying.

Menu suggestions. Start with any soup, homemade pasta, or **risotto**, or skip the pasta course and serve the stew accompanied by **po-lenta.** Fried Vegetables (page 69) such as zucchini, eggplant, or artichokes also make good accompani-ments.

Grow your own Italian herbs in olive oil contain-ers outdoors or in a sunny window inside.

Roast Chicken (Pollo Arrosto)

Classic roasted chicken is simplicity at its elegant best. Adapt the recipe with your favorite herbs and spices.

- **Salt and freshly ground black pepper to taste**
- **1 chicken, about 3 to 4 pounds, washed and dried**
- **4 whole cloves garlic, peeled**
- **4 sprigs parsley**
- **3 to 4 whole fresh** or **dried sage leaves**
- **1/4 cup vegetable oil**
- **3 tablespoons butter, softened**

1. Season chicken cavity with salt and pepper and add garlic, parsley, and sage. Place chicken in roasting pan containing the vegeta-ble oil. Spread butter over the top of the bird and sprinkle with salt and pepper. Set on a rack in a roasting pan, breast up.

2. Place in 350°F oven. Baste with pan drippings every 15 minutes and cook until skin is nicely browned, about 1 hour and 30 minutes **or** until thigh joint wiggles easily. Remove to heated platter.

3. Spoon off all but 1 table-spoon of the pan fat. Put the pan over medium-high heat, add a couple of table-spoons of water, and scrape residue from sides and bot-tom. Serve in a bowl to pour over the chicken after serv-ing. Serve hot, at room tem-perature, or cold (without the pan drippings) for **al fresco** dining.

Makes 4 servings.

Variations. Substitute rose-mary or bay leaves for the sage **or** prick 2 whole lemons all over with a fork, put inside cavity, and truss chicken (garlic is optional).

Menu suggestions. Roast chicken is one of those spe-cial dishes that goes with anything.

Chicken, Hunter's Style (Pollo alla Cacciatora)

An excellent version of one of the all-time favorite Italian dishes.

- **2 tablespoons olive oil**
- **1 2 1/2 to 3 pound chicken, cut up**
- **1 medium onion, sliced**
- **1 clove garlic, minced**
- **2 tablespoons minced parsley**
- **1 medium bell pepper, sliced**
- **1/2 pound fresh mushrooms, sliced**
- **1 cup Basic Tomato Sauce (page 36)** or **canned tomato sauce**
- **1/2 teaspoon dried oregano**
- **1/2 teaspoon dried basil**
- **1 bay leaf** **Salt and freshly ground black pepper to taste**
- **1/2 cup white wine**

1. In a large skillet, sauté chicken in olive oil until brown on all sides. Transfer to large ovenproof baking dish.

2. In same skillet, add onion, garlic, parsley, bell pepper, and mushrooms. Cook over medium heat until vegetables are tender,

about 5 to 8 minutes. Add more oil if necessary.

3. Blend in tomato sauce, herbs, and salt and pepper to taste. Heat through, then pour sauce over chicken. Cover with lid or aluminum foil and bake at 350° F for 45 minutes.

4. Remove cover, add wine, and cook for additional 15 minutes or until chicken is tender and sauce has thickened.

Makes 4 servings.

Menu suggestions. Serve on bed of spaghetti or other pasta with a sprinkling of grated Parmesan cheese. Accompany with a simple vegetable such as Braised Fennel (page 67) or Fried Vegetables (page 69).

Chicken Breasts Bolognese (Petti di Pollo alla Bolognese)

One of Italy's most delectable chicken dishes is prepared by the Bolognese. It is rich and wonderfully flavored with herbs and cheese.

8 split and boned chicken breasts (4 whole breasts), skin removed
Salt
½ cup butter
½ teaspoon oregano
½ teaspoon marjoram
1 teaspoon chopped parsley
¼ pound Bel Paese or imported fontina cheese
Flour
2 eggs, beaten
1 cup dried breadcrumbs
Cooking oil
½ cup dry white wine

1. Place each half breast between sheets of waxed paper; pound with a wooden mallet or rolling pin until flattened into cutlets about ⅛-inch thick. Sprinkle with salt.

2. Whip butter until fluffy; stir in herbs. Cut cheese lengthwise into 8 equal pieces. Spread half of the herbed butter mixture on the cheese pieces.

3. Place a stick of the cheese on each half breast. Roll up, tucking the ends of the chicken to seal tightly. Coat rolls with flour; dip into beaten eggs, then into breadcrumbs.

4. Fry in heavy skillet in ⅛-inch-deep layer vegetable oil over moderate heat until lightly browned; transfer to a flat, ovenproof baking dish.

5. Melt remaining herbed butter mixture in a saucepan; stir in wine and pour over chicken. Bake in a 375°F oven, basting occasionally, for about 15 minutes or until chicken is golden brown and tender. Serve with sauce spooned over top.

Makes 4 servings.

Menu suggestions. Serve with **Rissotto** with Mushrooms (page 48) and a simply prepared vegetable such as steamed asparagus laced with olive oil.

Chicken Breasts with Marsala (Petti di Pollo alla Marsala)

¼ cup flour
½ teaspoon salt
Freshly ground black pepper to taste
½ teaspoon dried oregano
2 large chicken breasts, halved and boned
3 teaspoons olive oil
3 tablespoons butter
½ cup Marsala wine

1. Combine flour, salt, pepper, and oregano. Dredge chicken breasts in mixture. Heat oil and butter in a heavy skillet. Brown chicken, cavity side first, until browned on both sides.

2. Add wine, cover, and simmer about ½ hour or until tender.

Serves 4.

Roast Stuffed Turkey (Tacchino Ripieno)

You may substitute duck, goose, chicken, Cornish game hens, or even quails for the turkey in this recipe—just adjust the amount of stuffing to the size of the fowl.

1 10- to 14-pound turkey, preferably fresh or thawed, if frozen
½ cup butter, room temperature
6 whole fresh or dried sage leaves
2 to 3 fresh or dried rosemary sprigs

1. Season turkey with salt and pepper inside and out. Stuff cavity loosely. Sew openings and truss securely. Spread the turkey with butter

and top with herbs. Place in a roasting pan, uncovered.

2. Cook at 325°F, allowing 25 minutes per pound, or until leg moves easily at the joint and breast feels springy to the touch. Baste occasionally with pan drippings or wine. If breast begins to get too brown, cover loosely with foil or a torn brown paper bag.

Makes 8 to 10 servings.

Turkey Stuffing

1 pound fresh chestnuts
2 cups homemade Chicken Broth (page 27) or regular-strength canned broth
2 tablespoons butter
1 cup chopped onion
1 cup chopped celery
1 cup ground sausage
2 cups soft, unseasoned breadcrumbs, soaked in milk then squeezed of excess moisture
2 apples, peeled, cored, and chopped
¼ pound dried pitted prunes, soaked in hot water to plump, then chopped (optional)
¼ cup chopped walnuts
2 eggs, lightly beaten
¼ cup freshly grated Parmesan cheese
⅓ cup chopped parsley
½ teaspoon crumbled dried sage
Salt and freshly ground black pepper to taste
1 cup dry white wine

1. Cut an "X" on flat side of chestnuts and cover with cold water in a saucepan. Bring to boil and cook 3 minutes. Remove from water and peel off shells and inner skins. Place peeled chestnuts in a pan, cover with chicken broth and simmer about 45 minutes, or until tender. Drain and chop coarsely. Reserve.

2. Heat butter over medium heat in a skillet and sauté onion and celery until soft. Add ground sausage and sauté 5 minutes, breaking up meat as finely as possible. Drain and discard fat.

3. In a large bowl, combine and mix chopped chestnuts, sausage-onion mixture, breadcrumbs, apples, prunes, walnuts, eggs, Parmesan cheese, parsley, sage, salt, pepper, and wine. Mixture should be moist, not wet. If it seems too dry, add more chicken broth.

Braised Squab (Piccionci in Umido)

Young pigeons raised commercially average about 1 pound and are served whole. For smaller appetites, split the birds in half. In lieu of usually expensive fresh squab, substitute Cornish game hens.

8 fresh squabs, well cleaned or 8 Cornish game hens
Salt and freshly ground black pepper
½ cup butter
1 cup dry white wine
½ cup flour
6 cups homemade Chicken Broth (page 27) or regular-strength canned broth, heated
1 teaspoon dried thyme
½ teaspoon dried sage
3 sprigs parsley
1 bay leaf
2 cups diced pancetta or lean salt pork (parboiled)
1 tablespoon butter
1 tablespoon olive oil
2 cloves garlic, minced
1 pound fresh mushrooms, sliced

1. Season cavities and outsides of squabs with salt and pepper.

2. Heat butter in large earthenware or other casserole over medium-high heat and brown the birds on all sides.

Remove and discard all but 2 tablespoons of the butter.

3. Add the wine to the remaining butter and cook until wine is evaporated. Blend in flour and stir until it begins to brown. Add stock or broth and stir until slightly thickened. Stir in herbs and **pancetta or salt pork.**

4. Place squabs in casserole and cover tightly. Cook over medium heat for about 20 to 30 minutes, turning frequently. Squabs are done if juices run clear when squab is pierced with a fork. (Cornish game hens require longer cooking time, about 1 hour.)

5. About 10 minutes before squabs are done, melt butter with olive oil in a large skillet and sauté garlic until slightly golden. Add mushrooms and sauté until tender, about 6 minutes.

6. Arrange on serving platter or individual plates and spoon resulting sauce over, garnishing with the sautéed mushrooms.

Makes 8 servings.

Skewered quail grilled over a charcoal fire are presented Italian style on a bed of polenta *prepared according to directions on page 52. Spinach Roman Style (page 68) is an exotically spiced accompaniment.*

Skewered Charcoal-Grilled Quail (Quaglie allo Spiedo)

If you don't have a hunter in the family, or access to a nearby quail farm, the little birds are now available frozen in many supermarkets.

8 quail, cleaned
Salt and freshly ground black pepper to taste
1 cup finely ground sausage
¼ cup chopped parsley
1 teaspoon crumbled dried sage
1 egg, beaten
8 slices bacon
¾ cup melted butter

1. Season quail cavities with salt and pepper.

2. Combine and mix well the sausage, parsley, sage, egg, and salt and pepper to taste. (**Do not** taste raw sausage mixture. To check seasonings, fry a tiny bit of sausage mixture until well cooked and taste that.) Stuff quail cavities. Wrap each bird with a strip of bacon and put 2 birds on each metal or wooden skewer.

3. Place on grill, about 5 inches above glowing coals. Brush with melted butter and roast until nicely browned, approximately 20 minutes, turning and basting occasionally with butter. Serve on a bed of **polenta**.

Makes 4 servings.

Variations. You may use the same technique for partridges, Cornish game hens, or other small fowl. Adjust cooking time and stuffing amount to the size of the birds.

Grilled Fish (Pesce alla Griglia)

One or more types of fresh fish may be used for this recipe. Cook in the broiler or grill over charcoal.

3 pounds fresh fish, cleaned and scaled, whole or in large pieces, washed and dried
⅓ cup olive oil
3 tablespoons freshly squeezed lemon juice
Salt and freshly ground black pepper to taste
1 bay leaf
Lemon wedges and parsley for garnish

1. Place fish in a shallow dish or pan containing a mixture of the olive oil, lemon juice, salt, pepper, and bay leaf. Marinate for 2 hours or more, turning fish several times to coat completely.

2. Cut a double piece of aluminum foil 2 inches longer and 2 inches wider than the fish. Turn the edges up 1 inch on all sides. Place the fish on the foil, then on hot grill about 5 inches from the heat source. Broil, basting occasionally with the marinade, until fish flakes easily and is done. Time will vary with the selected fish. By all means avoid overcooking. Serve hot, with plenty of lemon and parsley.

Makes 4 servings.

Menu suggestions. Keep the entire meal fish-oriented, if you wish, and start with a soup **or** pasta **or** risotto containing seafood, such as Fish Soup (page 29) or Shrimp **Risotto** (page 49). A crunchy vegetable salad is definitely in order as a follow-up, or even accompanying the fish, American-style.

Fish from American waters are quite different from the many species harvested from Italian seas. In the accompanying recipes, freely substitute whatever fresh fish are available in your locale.

Stuffed Striped Bass (Spigola Ripiena)

Although striped bass is the favored fish for this dish, any large, firm-fleshed fish can be substituted.

1 striped bass, weighing about 4 pounds
5 tablespoons olive oil
½ cup chopped celery
1 large onion, chopped
1 small clove garlic, chopped
2 cups breadcrumbs
1 teaspoon dried thyme
Pinch of marjoram
3 tablespoons freshly grated Parmesan cheese
Salt and freshly ground black pepper to taste
Juice of 1 lemon

1. Have fish cleaned, slit down center, and boned. Sprinkle inside with salt.

2. Prepare stuffing: Combine 3 tablespoons olive oil in a saucepan with celery, onion, and garlic; cook about 10 minutes or until vegetables are soft.

3. In a bowl, combine breadcrumbs with cooked vegetables, thyme, marjoram, Parmesan cheese, and salt and pepper to taste. Blend well. Stuff fish. Skewer or sew edges together to prevent stuffing from falling out. Place in a baking pan.

4. Brush fish with remaining 2 tablespoons oil. Cover pan with lid or foil and bake in 400° F oven for 10 minutes. Lower heat to 350° F and continue to bake for another 20 to 30 minutes or until fish is fork tender. If pan gets dry, add a small amount of hot water. Baste occasionally and add lemon juice just before serving.

Makes 6 servings.

Broiled Garlic Scampi (Scampi alla Griglia)

Unless you live where Italian **scampi** are imported to major fish markets, prepare this dish with jumbo shrimp or small lobster tails.

¼ cup olive oil
½ cup melted butter
¼ cup lemon juice
Salt and freshly ground black pepper to taste
3 tablespoons finely minced shallots
3 cloves garlic, finely minced
2 pounds scampi or jumbo prawns
Lemon slices and parsley for garnish

1. Combine olive oil, melted butter, lemon juice, salt, pepper, shallots, and garlic in a shallow baking dish. Add shrimp and turn several times to coat thoroughly.

2. Place dish of shrimp in preheated broiler about 4 inches from heat for about 5 minutes, turn and broil on the other side for 4 to 5 minutes longer; do not overcook. Pour resulting sauce from baking dish over shrimp. Garnish with lemon and sprinkle with parsley. Serve piping hot.

Makes 6 servings.

Menu suggestions. In small portions, this dish can be served as a hot appetizer. As a second course it follows well after any creamy rice or pasta dish that doesn't contain garlic. Green beans served at room temperature (see recipe on page 76) can move up from salad course to side dish with the shrimp.

Baked Oysters (Ostriche all' Italiana)

In small portions, baked oysters can be served as an appetizer. Prepare clams or mussels in the same manner.

3 tablespoons butter
2 to 3 cloves garlic, minced
1 cup Herb-Seasoned Breadcrumbs (page 71)
2 tablespoons chopped parsley
2 dozen small to medium-sized freshly shucked or canned oysters
¼ cup freshly grated Parmesan cheese

1. Melt 1 tablespoon butter in skillet over medium heat. Stir in garlic and breadcrumbs and cook until golden, about 3 minutes. Add parsley and stir.

2. Spread about ⅔ of the bread mixture on bottom of a buttered baking dish and arrange oysters on top in a single layer. Combine remaining breadcrumb mixture with the Parmesan cheese and spoon over top of oysters. Dot with 2 tablespoons butter and bake at 450° F until bubbling and golden brown on top. Serve piping hot.

Makes 6 servings.

Variations. If you shuck your own oysters, reserve shells. Wash and dry shells and arrange on a baking sheet. Distribute breadcrumb mixture among the shells. Top with an oyster, then more crumbs and butter. Bake as directed in the recipe. Serve on each individual plate.

Menu suggestions. Stuffed Pasta Rolls (page 47) get the meal off to an elegant start. Pasta with Peas and **Prosciutto** (page 67) is another fine alternative. No side vegetable dish is necessary, but you should serve a salad of mixed vegetables or greens after the oysters.

Stuffed Squid (Calamari Ripieni)

The sac-like body of this somewhat unattractive creature is perfect for stuffing. When cooked in tomato sauce, in the Sicilian manner, it is suddenly transformed into a very attractive and tasty dish.

2 pounds medium squid, cleaned as described in accompanying photographs, sacs only
2 cups Herb-Seasoned Breadcrumbs (page 71)
1 egg
3 tablespoons olive oil
2 whole cloves garlic
2 cups peeled and coarsely chopped fresh tomatoes or the equivalent in canned Italian-style plum tomatoes
Salt and freshly ground black pepper to taste
½ cup dry white wine
Chopped parsley for garnish

1. Rinse squid sacs well with cold water, drain, and dry with absorbent paper.

2. Combine breadcrumbs with egg and 1 tablespoon olive oil. Fill squid sacs ⅔ full with crumb mixture. Close open ends with toothpicks.

3. Heat the remaining 2 tablespoons olive oil in a 4-quart Dutch oven or large saucepan. Add the whole garlic and fry for 5 minutes. Remove and discard the garlic. Add squid to the pan and brown on all sides. Stir in the tomatoes, reduce heat to low, cover, and simmer gently for 25 minutes.

4. Add salt and pepper to taste, and white wine. Cook for an additional 5 minutes. Transfer squid to a warmed platter. Remove the toothpicks. Slice the squid crosswise into rings and arrange neatly on the platter. Pour over the sauce and garnish with chopped parsley.

Makes 6 servings.

Menu suggestions. This dish, when served with plain boiled spaghetti, is a meal in itself. A crisp, mixed green salad and Mixed Fruit Compote (page 80) complete the menu.

Fried Squid (Calamari Fritti)

Most local fish markets now sell squid (**calamari**) fresh or frozen. Frying is a favorite Italian way to enjoy the delicate flavor.

2 pounds fresh squid or frozen, thawed, cleaned as described on page 24, and cut into rings
1 cup flour
1 cup Herb-Seasoned Breadcrumbs (page 71)
Vegetable oil for frying
Salt and freshly ground black pepper to taste
Lemon wedges or white wine vinegar
Chopped parsley for garnish

1. Combine flour and breadcrumbs. Coat squid with this mixture, shaking off excess.

2. Heat vegetable oil in a deep frying pan to a depth of about 2 inches. Fry rings a few at a time until lightly browned, about 30 seconds. Do not overcook or squid will be tough.

3. Drain well and keep warm while you finish frying all the pieces. Add salt and pepper and serve with lemon wedges or wine vinegar to sprinkle on top, if desired. Garnish with parsley.

Makes 4 to 6 servings.

Menu suggestions. Precede with **fettuccine** or other noodles tossed in **Pesto** Sauce (page 36) or Fresh Tomato and Basil sauce (page 37). Present the squid on a bed of fried potatoes or combine with other fried fish, chicken, meats, and assorted vegetables for a mixed fry.

Under running water, pull off the speckled membrane from squid, then gently separate sac or hood from tentacles. Pull out sword or shell from inside the hood as shown in the top photograph and rinse inside of hood. Pat dry and set aside. Slice horizontally just above the eyes (lower left) and discard everything except the tentacles. Slice the hood into rings (lower left) for frying or marinating (see page 24), or retain whole sacs for stuffing as in the recipe to the left.

Scallops Sautéed in Garlic (Conchiglie alla Griglia)

Vary this recipe by combining part scallops with crab meat and shelled prawns or shrimp for a mixed seafood sauté. Or cook squid in this manner after cleaning and slicing into rings, as described on page 24.

2 cloves garlic, crushed
¼ cup butter
2 pounds scallops, cut into bite-sized pieces
Salt and freshly ground black pepper to taste
¾ cup dry white wine or sherry
Chopped parsley for garnish

1. Sauté garlic in butter in a frying pan over medium heat until garlic browns. Remove garlic. Add scallops and sauté about 3 minutes, turning on all sides. Season with salt and pepper. Cover pan, reduce heat, and cook about 5 minutes longer.

2. Remove scallops to heated platter. Turn up heat to high, add wine, and quickly reduce pan drippings and wine to about ½ their original quantity. Remove from heat, pour over scallops, and garnish with chopped parsley. Serve immediately.

Makes 6 servings.

Menu Suggestions. Basic Risotto with Parmesan (page 48) is a marvelous complimentary flavor. Serve as a first course or, American style, along with the scallops. Lightly cooked and mildly seasoned green vegetables such as asparagus, zucchini, or broccoli would be appropriate side dishes.

Spinach and Cheese Pie (Torta di Ricotta)

Italian cooks often make spinach pie at Eastertime. You'll find it's worth making all year long.

Pastry

3 cups flour
1 cup butter, cut into small pieces
6½ teaspoon salt

2 egg yolks
3 tablespoons cold water
1 egg white, lightly beaten (reserved)

Filling

2 cups finely chopped onion
3 tablespoons olive oil
2 pounds fresh spinach, cooked, drained, and chopped or 20 ounces frozen chopped spinach, cooked according to package directions and well drained
1½ cups freshly grated Parmesan cheese
1 cup ricotta cheese
4 eggs, lightly beaten
2 cups diced ham
Salt and freshly ground black pepper to taste

1. If using food processor, place flour, butter, and salt in food processor bowl and blend with steel knife for a few seconds until mixture resembles oatmeal. Add yolks and water and process until ball is formed. Wrap in waxed paper and chill briefly, while you prepare filling. (Pastry can, of course, be traditionally prepared using pastry blender, knives, or fingertips.)

2. To make filling, sauté onion in olive oil until tender, but not browned. Add to the cooked drained spinach. Cool before stirring in Parmesan cheese, **ricotta**, eggs, ham, salt, and pepper.

3. Roll half of the pastry and line a 10-inch tart pan with removable bottom. Brush interior surfaces with egg white. Add filling.

4. Roll remaining pastry and position on top of filling; seal and flute edges. Cut a center hole for steam to escape. If desired, cut flowers, leaves, or other shapes from pastry scraps and decorate top crust.

5. Bake at 425°F until crust is golden, about 40 minutes. Cool 15 to 20 minutes before removing from pan.

Makes 8 servings.

Note. The pie reheats well in a microwave oven or loosely covered with foil in a conventional oven at 375°F. It can be kept frozen for several weeks.

Italian Spinach Omelet (Frittata di Spinaci)

Open-faced Italian omelets are cooked on both sides in a round skillet over very low heat until firm. They may be eaten immediately or at room temperature. A **frittata** can be filled with almost anything you have on hand—cooked meats, cheeses, herbs, seafood, vegetables. Create your own favorite version based on the suggestions that follow the basic recipe.

6 eggs
2 tablespoons cream
¼ cup freshly grated Parmesan cheese
Salt and freshly ground black pepper
1 pound fresh spinach, cleaned, washed, and drained or 1 10-ounce package frozen chopped spinach, thawed, briefly cooked, and drained
1 tablespoon olive oil
1 tablespoon butter
2 cloves garlic, minced
½ cup chopped onion
Parsley for garnish (optional)

1. In a bowl, beat eggs with cream, cheese, and salt and pepper to taste.

2. Cook the fresh spinach for about 2 minutes in water that clings from washing. Drain well and chop coarsely.

3. In a 12-inch skillet in which foods do not stick, combine ½ the butter and the olive oil. Over medium heat, sauté garlic and onion until golden. Distribute spinach evenly in the pan and pour in the egg and cheese mixture. Immediately turn heat to lowest position.

4. Cook omelet undisturbed until eggs are set around the edges, then gently lift edges of the omelet with a spatula and tilt the pan to let uncooked egg run down under the bottom. Continue cooking until eggs have almost set on top. Place a plate over the top of the pan, invert to turn **frittata** onto the plate. Add remaining butter to the pan and slide the **frittata** back into the pan with the cooked side up. Cook for another 2 to 3 minutes to set bottom. (Instead of turning the **frittata**, you can place it under a preheated broiler for 20 to 30 seconds to set the top; but be careful not to burn or overcook.)

5. Again place a plate over the pan, invert, and turn **frittata** out onto the preheated serving plate, or loosen edges with a spatula and slide the **frittata** onto the plate. Garnish with parsley, if desired.

Makes 4 servings.

Vegetable variations. Instead of spinach, substitute about 1½ cups of any one or a combination of the following and cook the frittata in the same way:

Artichokes. Cleaned and cut into wedges as for Fried Vegetables (page 69) and simmered in a little water until tender or frozen artichoke hearts, thawed, chopped, and briefly sautéed.

Asparagus. Cooked until just tender but still crisp in boiling salted water, then cut into bite-sized lengths.

Broccoli. Steamed and sliced into bite-sized pieces.

Eggplant. Diced and sautéed or steamed or boiled until tender.

Green beans. Cooked until just tender but still crisp in boiling salted water, then coarsely chopped.

Onion. Sliced or chopped and sautéed in butter or olive oil until soft.

Canned Italian-style plum tomatoes. Very well drained and chopped.

Zucchini. Chopped and steamed or sautéed in olive oil.

Grated Parmesan, jack, or other favorite cheeses.

Menu suggestions. Frittata may be cut into small portions and served hot or at room temperature as appetizers. Wrap **frittata** in foil to take along on picnics.

Italian-style omelets are among the easiest dishes of the entire cuisine to prepare. Possibilities for fillings are limited only by your imagination and available ingredients. Serve the frittata *in the skillet or invert onto a platter. Unlike other omelets, a* frittata *can be delicious cold or reheated.*

Vegetables (Verdura)

The extraordinary variety of high quality fresh produce found in Italy is often not available in American markets. To ensure flavorful vegetable dishes, buy only what is fresh in the market and choose recipes or improvise accordingly.

Stuffed Artichokes (Carciofi Ripieni)

The most dramatic Italian vegetable dish is probably stuffed artichokes, their leaves bulging with well-seasoned breadcrumbs. Tomato sauce keeps them moist during baking and makes an excellent dip in which to dunk the filled leaves.

2 medium-sized artichokes, prepared according to following directions
1½ cups Herb-Seasoned Breadcrumbs, (page 71)
1 hardcooked egg, chopped
2 anchovy filets, finely chopped
Salt and freshly ground black pepper to taste
2 teaspoons olive oil
1 cup Basic Tomato Sauce or canned tomato sauce
¼ cup freshly grated Parmesan cheese

1. Prepare artichokes as directed below.
2. Combine breadcrumbs, egg, anchovy, and salt and pepper to taste.
3. Stuff the prepared filling into center cavity of the artichokes; fill bewteen leaves with a teaspoon. Drizzle 1 teaspoon olive oil over each artichoke.
4. In a greased, shallow 9-inch baking dish, pour ½ of the tomato sauce. Stand artichokes in the dish and pour the rest of the sauce over them. Sprinkle with cheese, and cover with foil.
5. Bake at 350°F for 20 to 30 minutes. Remove the foil for the last few minutes of cooking and allow the sauce to thicken. Artichokes are done when the hearts can be pierced easily with a metal skewer or long-tined fork.
Makes 2 servings.

Stuffed Artichokes are among the showiest of all Italian-style vegetable dishes. They can be a first course, vegetable side dish, or even a main dish for an American-style light lunch or supper.

How to prepare artichokes for stuffing

Wash artichokes well in cold running water, making sure you have cleaned any dirt from between the leaves. Cut off small, dark outer leaves and slice a ¾-inch piece off the pointed top. With kitchen shears or a sharp knife, trim ¾-inch from each leaf to remove thorn. Slice off stem evenly at base to allow artichoke to stand without tipping over.

Fill large saucepan with 4 quarts of water and add ½ lemon, sliced. Bring to a rapid boil and add artichokes. Cook over medium-high heat for approximately 15 minutes, or until leaves pull free easily. Add water during cooking, if necessary. Avoid overcooking; artichokes should not be mushy. Remove from water, drain upside down, and allow to cool.

To make a cavity for stuffing, gently pull out tender center leaves with a teaspoon, scrape out and remove fuzzy inner choke at the cavity's bottom.

Menu suggestions. For a light lunch or supper, precede with a soup and follow with fresh fruit. Or serve artichokes as a first course with almost anything. Small artichokes make good accompaniments to simply prepared meats or fowls.

Whether harvested from the garden or purchased at the local market, vegetables should be fresh.

Asparagus Parmesan (Asparagi alla Parmigiana)

Perk up any springtime feast with this simple dish.

2 pounds fresh, tender, young asparagus
Salt
½ cup freshly grated Parmesan cheese
6 tablespoons butter, melted

1. Break off and discard tough asparagus ends. Peel lower part of stalk, if desired. Wash and cook in boiling salted water until tender but crisp to the bite. Drain well.

2. Place asaparagus in layered rows in a buttered baking dish, sprinkling each layer with cheese and butter before adding the next layer.

3. Bake in a 450° F oven until cheese and butter form a golden crust.

Makes 4 servings.

Variation. Top asparagus with poached or fried eggs for a light main dish.

Eggplant Parmesan (Melanzane alla Parmigiana)

2 medium eggplants, peeled
Salt
Flour
Olive oil
2 cups Basic Tomato Sauce (page 36)
8 ounces mozzarella cheese, coarsely grated
½ cup freshly grated Parmesan cheese
3 tablespoons butter

1. Cut eggplant horizontally in ½-inch slices. Sprinkle both sides lightly with salt and place on paper towels. Cover with more paper towels and place a wooden board or heavy weight on top for 30 minutes to withdraw moisture. Rinse and pat dry with paper towels. Dredge with flour and fry slices in shallow olive oil in a heavy pan over medium-high heat until lightly browned, adding oil as necessary. Salt to taste and drain on paper towels.

2. Place a single layer of fried eggplant in a buttered baking dish. Cover with ⅓ of the tomato sauce, ⅓ of the **mozzarella** cheese, and ⅓ of the Parmesan cheese. Continue layering eggplant, sauce, and cheese for two more layers, ending up with Parmesan on the top. Dot with butter and bake at 400°F for about 30 minutes.

Makes 4 servings.

Mushrooms Parmesan (Funghi alla Parmigiana)

Large mushroom caps filled with a savory bread stuffing are elegant, yet easy to prepare.

1 pound large mushrooms
2 cloves garlic, finely minced
2 tablespoons finely minced parsley
3 tablespoons grated Parmesan cheese
1 teaspoon oregano
½ cup breadcrumbs
½ cup olive oil
Salt and pepper to taste

1. Wash mushrooms and remove the stems, wipe dry. Chop stems and mix with garlic, parsley, cheese, oregano, breadcrumbs, salt and pepper.

2. Place mushroom caps cavity-side-up in an oiled shallow baking dish. Fill the cavities with the chopped mixture and fill the bottom of the baking dish with water to a depth of ¼ inch. Pour the olive oil evenly over the caps.

3. Bake in 350° F oven for 30 minutes. Serve hot.

Note. Smaller mushroom caps can be prepared in the same manner and served as an appetizer.

Green Beans with Tomato and Garlic (Fagiolini all' Pomodoro)

Green beans can be cooked ahead and reheated just before serving.

½ cup olive oil
1 small onion, chopped
2 cloves garlic, minced
1 tablespoon chopped fresh sage leaves, chopped fresh or ½ teaspoon crumbled dried whole sage leaves
2 pounds green beans, trimmed, washed, and cut into small pieces
3 cups canned or peeled fresh Italian-style plum tomatoes
Salt and freshly ground black pepper to taste
Water

1. Heat oil in saucepan over medium-high heat and sauté onion, garlic, and sage until wilted. Add green beans and tomatoes, along with salt and pepper and just enough water to barely cover. Bring to boil, cover, and reduce heat.

2. Cook, stirring occasionally, until beans are tender, about 30 minutes.

Makes 6 servings.

Peas with Eggs (Uova e Piselli)

This is a simple dish that might be served in an Italian home as a light lunch or late Sunday supper.

- 4 **tablespoons olive oil**
- 1 **large onion, chopped**
- 1 **cup quartered canned Italian-style plum tomatoes**
- ½ **teaspoon dried basil**
- ½ **cup fresh** or **frozen green peas**
  Salt and freshly ground black pepper to taste
- 6 **eggs**

1. Heat oil in a large shallow saucepan or frying pan; add onion and cook about 2 minutes or until onion is transparent. Stir in tomatoes and basil and simmer for 15 minutes. Add peas, salt and pepper, and simmer for an additional 10 minutes.

2. Make six indentations in the sauce with the back of a spoon. Drop one egg into each indentation, being careful not to break the yolks. Sprinkle with salt and pepper and cook slowly about 3 minutes, or until eggs are done. Adjust seasoning if necessary.

Makes 6 servings.

Italian Fried Peppers (Peperoni all' Oglio)

Choose large sweet red or green bell peppers for this popular Italian vegetable dish.

- 4 **large firm sweet peppers**
- 2 **tablespoons olive oil**
- 2 **tablespoons butter**
- 1 **clove garlic, crushed**
- 1½ **teaspoons salt**
- ⅛ **teaspoon freshly ground black pepper**
- 1 **teaspoon oregano**

1. Wash peppers, remove stems and seeds. Cut lengthwise into strips about 1½-inches wide.

2. Heat oil and butter in a large frying pan. Add peppers and garlic and cook over medium heat until lightly browned, stirring occasionally. Sprinkle with salt, pepper, and oregano. Cover and cook on low heat for 15 minutes.

Makes 4 servings.

Sautéed Mushrooms (Funghi Trifolati)

Marketplaces in Italy offer a colorful array of fresh mushrooms that are prepared and served as appetizers, side dishes, or even second courses.

- 1 **pound fresh mushrooms**
- 1 **clove garlic, minced**
- 2 **tablespoons olive oil**
- 1 **tablespoon butter**
- ¼ **cup dry white wine**
- 1 **tablespoon lemon juice**
  Salt and freshly ground black pepper
- 3 **tablespoons chopped parsley**

1. Clean mushrooms in a solution of salt and water. Discard slice from stem end. Slice very thinly, crosswise.

2. Sauté garlic in olive oil and butter over medium-high heat until lightly golden. Adjust heat to high, add mushrooms and sauté until oil is absorbed. Reduce heat, add wine and lemon juice, salt and pepper, and cook a few minutes more, until tender. Stir in parsley, pour into preheated dish, and serve immediately. Or serve at room temperature as an **antipasto.**

Makes about 4 servings.

Braised Fennel (Finocchi all' Olio)

- 3 **large sweet fennel bulbs**
- ½ **cup olive oil**
  Salt

1. Remove and discard damaged or wilted outside part of the fennel, as well as tops and a slice off the bottom of the bulbs. Cut bulbs into vertical slices and wash in cold water.

2. Place fennel slices, olive oil, and water to barely cover in a saucepan. Cook over medium heat, uncovered, until fork tender, about 30 to 40 minutes, stirring occasionally. If it becomes dry, add a bit of hot water. Add salt to taste and serve on preheated platter.

Makes 4 servings.

Broccoli Sautéed with Garlic (Broccoli all' Aglio)

Italian vegetables are often partially cooked in water until almost tender, then sautéed in olive oil and/or butter.

- 1 **bunch fresh broccoli** or **2 10-ounce packages frozen sliced broccoli**
- 2 **cloves garlic, minced**
- ¼ **cup olive oil**
  Salt to taste

1. Slice off and discard ends of fresh broccoli stalks, peel stalks if broccoli is tough. Split stalks in two or into quarters with florets left attached. Or slice whole stalks horizontally into bite-sized pieces. Steam or drop into boiling salted water and cook until just fork tender. Drain well. (Cook frozen broccoli according to package directions until barely tender.)

2. Over medium heat, sauté garlic in olive oil until golden. Add broccoli and salt and sauté about 3 to 4 minutes.

Makes 4 servings.

Peas Sautéed with Prosciutto (Piselli al Prosciutto)

A wonderful way to prepare green peas.

- 2 **tablespoons olive oil**
- 2 **small cloves garlic, peeled**
- ½ **small white onion, finely chopped**
- 3 **tablespoons diced** prosciutto or pancetta or **bacon** or **salt pork**
- 2 **pounds tiny fresh peas, shelled** or **1 10-ounce package tiny frozen peas, thawed**
- 2 **tablespoons minced parsley**
  Salt and freshly ground black pepper

1. Heat olive oil in skillet over medium heat and sauté garlic until browned. Remove and discard garlic cloves. Add onion and pork and sauté until onions are tender.

2. Add peas and cook until they are just tender, about 5 minutes (if peas seem dry during cooking, add a little water, white wine, or chicken broth). Toss in parsley and add salt and pepper to taste.

Makes 4 servings.

Spinach Roman Style (Spinaci alla Romana)

Raisins and pine nuts add an exotic touch to this spinach dish.

2 **bunches fresh spinach, well washed and trimmed**
3 **tablespoons olive oil**
2 **cloves garlic, minced**
¼ **pound thinly sliced** prosciutto, **shredded**
2 **tablespoons white raisins**
2 **tablespoons pine nuts** or **blanched slivered almonds**
3 **tablespoons butter**
Salt and freshly ground black pepper to taste

1. Cook spinach in covered saucepan, in only the water that clings to the leaves from washing, until tender. Drain, pressing out all liquid.

2. Sauté spinach in olive oil with garlic and **prosciutto** until garlic is lightly browned. Add raisins, pine nuts, and butter. Stir until butter melts, then add seasonings to taste.

Makes 4 servings.

Baked Stuffed Tomatoes (Pomodori Ripieni)

Serve as a side dish **(contorno)** with roasted or grilled meats while still warm, or when cold as an **antipasto**.

8 **large ripe tomatoes**
Salt and freshly ground black pepper to taste
1 **cup finely chopped onion**
¼ **cup olive oil**
6 **anchovy filets, rinsed and finely chopped**
2 **tablespoons tiny capers**
2 **cups Herb-Seasoned Breadcrumbs (page 71)**
⅓ **cup pine nuts, ground in food processor (optional)**
¼ **cup minced parsley**
½ **cup freshly grated Parmesan cheese**
¼ **cup butter**

1. Cut slice off bottoms of tomatoes (the flat top of a tomato makes a firmer base). Scoop out seed and center pulp into a sieve and collect juices; reserve. Season tomato cavities with salt and pepper to taste and place them in an oiled baking dish.

2. Sauté onion in olive oil until golden.

3. Combine onion and pan drippings with anchovies, capers, breadcrumbs, pine nuts, parsley, Parmesan cheese, and reserved tomato juices. Taste, and add salt and pepper as required.

4. Fill tomatoes with stuffing mixture. Dot with butter and bake at 400° F until tomatoes are tender but still hold their shape, about 10 to 15 minutes.

Makes 8 servings.

Vegetable Flan (Sformato di Verdura)

This dish, similar to a souffle, is very versatile and can be made with whatever fresh vegetables are available from the garden or market. Different combinations can be used to achieve varying colors—green vegetables only; a mixture of carrots, celery, and cauliflower; or a mixed garden bouquet.

½ **pound cooked vegetables, well drained (green beans, carrots, celery, cauliflower, spinach)**
1 **cup milk**
1 **cup heavy cream**
4 **eggs**
¼ **cup flour**
¼ **cup freshly grated Parmesan cheese**
Salt to taste
Freshly ground black pepper and nutmeg to taste

1. Put cooked vegetables through food processor or purée in blender; mix with remaining ingredients.

2. Butter 8 individual 1-cup molds or ramekins and distribute vegetable mixture evenly, using ¾ cup mixture for each mold.

3. Bake at 375° F for 30 minutes or until set. Serve immediately.

Makes 8 servings.

Zucchini Genoa Style (Zucchini alla Genovese)

In the peak of summer, when zucchini is plentiful and garden fresh herbs abound, the Genovese combine them in this tasty oven baked **frittata**.

6 **to 8 young, tender zucchini**
¼ **cup olive oil**
1 **medium onion, sliced**
½ **cup diced green pepper**
1 **tablespoon minced parsley**
1 **clove garlic, minced**
6 **eggs, beaten**
¼ **cup finely chopped fresh basil**
½ **cup grated Parmesan cheese**
Salt and freshly ground black pepper to taste

1. Wash and thinly slice the zucchini. Heat the olive oil in a large skillet and add zucchini, onion, bell pepper, parsley, and garlic. Cook over medium heat until zucchini is tender. Remove from heat and set aside to cool.

2. To the beaten eggs, add the fresh basil and Parmesan cheese. Add the zucchini mixture and blend together. Add salt and pepper to taste (the cheese may be salty).

3. Grease an 8-inch square baking dish and turn the zucchini mixture into it. Bake at 400° F for 25 minutes or until the top is golden in color and a knife comes out clean when inserted in the center. Serve hot or at room temperature. Can be made ahead and reheated.

Makes 6 servings.

Stuffed Zucchini (Zucchini Ripieni)

The flavor of stuffed zucchini improves when reheated, making it an excellent prepare-ahead dish. Stuffed zucchini may also be served as a first course.

6 **medium zucchini, well scrubbed**
¼ **cup olive oil**
⅔ **cup chopped onion**
1 **tablespoon minced garlic**
½ **pound ground lean beef** or **veal**
¼ **cup chopped** prosciutto or pancetta or **ham**
2 **tablespoons tomato paste**
1 **egg, beaten**
⅔ **cup soft white bread crumbs, without crusts**
½ **cup freshly grated Parmesan cheese**
2 **tablespoons chopped parsley**
1 **tablespoon chopped fresh oregano** or **1 teaspoon crumbled dried oregano**
Salt and freshly ground black pepper to taste

1. Cut zucchini in half lengthwise and scoop out most of the pulp to leave a ¼-inch thick shell. Coarsely chop pulp and reserve; set shells aside.

2. Heat oil in a skillet over medium heat and sauté onion until soft. Add garlic and reserved zucchini pulp and sauté about 5 minutes more. Drain well in a sieve or colander.

3. Combine drained zucchini mixture with remaining ingredients, cool, then mix well with hands.

4. Place hollowed zucchini in an oiled baking dish side by side. Fill cavities with the stuffing mixture. Sprinkle with additional grated Parmesan and dot with butter, if desired. Bake at 375° F until zucchini is tender, but not mushy, and stuffing is lightly browned, about 30 minutes or longer. (If tops are getting too browned, cover loosely with foil during cooking.) Serve warm, but not piping hot.

Makes 6 servings.

Fried Vegetables (Sauté di Verdura Mista)

Vegetables may be fried in the Italian manner, one kind at a time, or in combination, or be included in a mixed fry (**fritto misto**), which is a combination of fried boneless veal, chicken, calves brains, liver, and other organ meat. The procedure for cooking is the same.

Heat enough vegetable oil for deep frying in a heavy pan over high heat until the oil is very hot. Add prepared vegetables (as described below) and fry until golden brown, from 3 to 6 minutes.

Artichokes are fried over medium heat in a shallow heavy skillet, with oil to a depth of only 1 to 2 inches, turned until all sides are golden and crusty. (Any vegetables can be fried in the shallow skillet method as an alternative to deep frying.)

After vegetables are cooked, remove from oil with a slotted spoon and drain on paper towels before serving. Add salt and pepper to taste. Vegetables may be sprinkled just before eating with a little vinegar or fresh lemon juice, but don't let them sit this way or they will get soggy. As you will note in the following directions for vegetable preparation, some require blanching or partial cooking prior to frying.

Whole Artichokes (Carciofi alla Guidia)

Select small or medium artichokes. Leaving stems attached, snap off the tough lower leaves. Then, using scissors, cut off the outer part of the remaining leaves, leaving only the whitish edible part. As you work up the choke, the edible portion becomes longer, and the artichoke begins to look like a rosebud. When you reach the core of leaves in the center, slice them off to eliminate the green tips. Then scoop out the fuzzy interior choke.

With a sharp knife or vegetable peeler, pare lower part of the outside leaves, base, and stem to expose the white portion. Cut the stem to form a short stump. Rub all cut parts with lemon to avoid discoloration.

Gently spread leaves out as much as possible without breaking them, lay artichoke against work surface, and flatten gently with your hand. Salt and pepper outside and inside cavity.

Fry over medium heat using the shallow skillet method outlined above. Turn several times and cook until bottoms pierce easily with a fork, about 15 minutes. Have a second skillet ready, with oil heated very hot over high heat. Place artichokes in stem-side up and fry until golden.

Artichoke Pieces (Carciofini Fritti)

Prepare raw artichokes as above, then cut into small wedges vertically. Drop into boiling water containing a little lemon juice and cook until just tender, approximately 6 minutes. Drain and cool before dipping into beaten egg, then fine breadcrumbs. Fry until all sides are golden and crusty. (Frozen artichoke hearts can be fried by first thawing completely, patting dry, and dipping into the egg and breadcrumbs.)

Asparagus (Asparagi Fritti)

Break off stem to within 4 inches of the tip, discard bottom stem. Wash and pat dry. Dip into beaten egg, then fine breadcrumbs, and fry a few stalks at a time.

Cauliflower (Cavofiore Fritto)

Boil whole cauliflower until just barely fork tender. Cool and break into florets and cut these into bite-sized pieces. Dip into beaten egg, then fine seasoned breadcrumbs before frying.

Outdoor markets in Italy abound in fresh vegetables that would make any cook envious. Choose an assortment for Fried Vegetables or prepare the kind that's most available in the garden or at the greengrocer.

Eggplant (Melanzane Fritte)

Peel and slice eggplants lengthwise about ½-inch thick. Sprinkle with salt and place in a large colander and set aside for 30 minutes to draw out excess moisture. Dry with paper towel and slice into chunky strips. No breadcrumbs or flour are required, although you may lightly dust with flour before frying.

Green Beans (Fagiolini Fritti)

Cut off tips and trim beans. Cook in salted boiling water until almost done, about 20 minutes. Cool. Tie in small bundles with string and dip bundles into beaten egg, then flour. Fry, and remove string before serving.

Tomatoes (Pomodori Fritti)

Wash green or firm ripe tomatoes, slice horizontally ½-inch thick, and gently remove seeds, if desired. Dredge in flour, then dip in beaten egg, and finally into fine seasoned breadcrumbs. Fry until crusty.

Zucchini (Zucchini Fritti)

Clean (if soil is embedded in skin) or peel zucchini, and cut lengthwise into thin strips as you would prepare potatoes for frying. Salt strips and allow to sit for about 30 minutes, then drain and pat dry. Dip into flour and fry a few at a time.

In every Italian or Italian-American community there's at least one good bakery where you can find crusty bread baked daily or seasonal baked specialties.

Breads and Snacks (Pane e Svogliature)

Italian cooks rely on the local bakery for their breads. Every village in Italy has a great baker, and Italian-American communities have at least one good bakery for daily supplies of fresh breads.

You'll want good, crusty Italian bakery-fresh loaves or breadsticks for most of your Italian meals. If there are no Italian bakeries nearby, crusty French bread is a good substitute, and is usually easier to find. When you do find a good Italian loaf, buy several and store them in the freezer.

Save sweet breads for special occasions or eat them whenever you like. Breadlike snacks (*svogliature*) can be eaten anytime or served as appetizers.

Garlic Bread (Bruschetta)

We should learn to call this "Garlic and Olive Oil Bread," because good quality fruity green olive oil is even more important than the garlic.

Cut a fresh loaf of crusty Italian or French bread into thick slices, leaving slices still attached to the loaf at the bottom. Toast the sliced loaf in the oven at 350° F until golden brown and crispy. Rub the sides of the hot slices with plenty of freshly peeled crushed garlic, and brush or drizzle with olive oil. Sprinkle with salt and freshly ground pepper to taste.

When you have something on the charcoal grill or barbeque, slice a loaf of bread and rub both sides of each slice with garlic. Brush with olive oil and grill each side until toasted.

Drizzle on more olive oil and add salt and freshly ground black pepper to taste. Enjoy while waiting for the rest of the meal to cook.

70

Rosemary and Raisin Bread (Pane al Rosmarino)

Frozen bread dough makes this an easy treat to accompany soups or salads. Sliced, it is good breakfast toast.

1 tablespoon chopped fresh rosemary leaves, or 1 teaspoon dried crumbled rosemary leaves
1 pound frozen yeast dough, thawed or your own favorite bread dough made from about 3 cups flour, risen once
3 tablespoons olive oil
½ cup golden raisins, soaked in warm water

1. Sauté rosemary in olive oil until very hot, but not browned. Remove from heat and reserve.

2. Place dough on lightly floured smooth surface. Make a hollow in the middle and pour in the rosemary and 2 tablespoons oil. (If you wish, the rosemary can be strained and discarded, leaving only the flavored oil.) Work thoroughly into the dough. Add raisins and knead them into the dough.

3. Shape into a round loaf, or break apart and form into a dozen small buns. Place on a greased baking sheet. Brush tops with remaining 1 tablespoon oil. Slash an "X" with a sharp knife on the top of the loaf or buns, and cover with plastic wrap or waxed paper. Let stand in a warm place until well risen.

4. Bake at 350° F until browned, about 15 minutes for buns, 20 to 35 minutes for loaf.

Makes 1 loaf or 12 buns.

Panettone

Milanese bakers use a special mold to bake this bread-like coffee cake. Lacking molds, Italian-Americans learned to substitute coffee cans or paper bags. Panettone is eaten all year round, but especially during the Christmas season.

¾ cup milk, scalded
1 package active dry yeast
¼ cup warm water (105° to 115° F)
½ cup butter
½ cup sugar
3 eggs
2 teaspoons grated lemon rind
1 teaspoon salt
1 teaspoon anise seed
1 teaspoon anise extract
3½ to 4 cups all-purpose flour
¼ cup golden raisins
¼ cup coarsely chopped citron
½ cup pine nuts
Melted butter

1. Scald milk and set aside to cool.

2. Sprinkle yeast into warm water and let stand until dissolved.

3. In large bowl of electric mixer, cream butter until soft, add sugar, and beat until fluffy and light. Beat in eggs one at a time. Add yeast mixture, milk, lemon rind, salt, anise seed, and anise extract.

4. Add 1 cup flour and beat for 3 minutes. Using a wooden spoon or wire whisk, gradually beat in the remaining flour, adding only enough to make a soft dough. Mix in raisins, citron, and pine nuts.

5. Turn dough out on lightly floured board and knead until smooth and no longer sticky, about 10 to 12 minutes. Place dough in a greased bowl, cover, and let rise until doubled in bulk, about 1½ hours.

6. Turn out again onto floured board and knead lightly. Place dough in a greased and flour-dusted panettone mold or 2 greased 1-pound coffee cans. (Or generously butter 2 brown paper bags (use the No. 6 lunchbag size), each with its top folded down to form a 3-inch cuff.) Cover and let rise until double in size.

7. Brush tops with melted butter. Bake at 350° F until golden brown, 30 to 40 minutes. To serve hot, tear off bag (or remove can) and cut bread in wedges. To serve cold, wrap bread (still in bag or can) first in a clean cloth, then in foil and let cool completely.

Makes 2 loaves.

Sweet Bread Rings (Buccelati)

Anise-flavored buccelati store well in the freezer. Reheat thawed rings by wrapping in foil and placing in a warm oven.

½ cup golden raisins
3 tablespoons Marsala wine
1 package active dry yeast
1 teaspoon sugar
¼ cup warm water (105° to 115° F)
½ cup milk
½ cup butter
1 teaspoon salt
½ cup sugar
2 teaspoons grated orange rind
2 tablespoons orange juice
2 teaspoons anise seed
1 teaspoon anise extract
3 eggs (reserve 1 white)
3½ to 4 cups unsifted all-purpose flour
Orange Glaze (recipe follows)

1. Combine raisins and Marsala and set aside.

2. Sprinkle yeast and 1 teaspoon sugar into warm water, let stand until dissolved, about 10 minutes.

3. In a small saucepan, over medium heat, combine milk, butter, salt, ½ cup sugar, orange rind and juice, and anise seed. Heat just until butter is melted. Pour mixture into a large bowl; cool slightly, add anise extract.

4. Stir in yeast mixture. Add eggs 1 at a time (reserve 1 white for later use), beating well after each addition. Add Marsala, which has been strained from reserved raisins.

5. Add 1½ cups flour to the mixture and beat well with a wooden spoon or wire whisk. Continue to beat for 3 minutes. Gradually add remaining flour, adding only enough to make a soft dough. Beat well after each addition.

6. Turn out on a lightly floured board and knead until smooth and satiny, about 12 to 15 minutes. Sprinkle raisins on dough and knead them evenly into the dough. Place in a bowl, cover, and let rise in a warm place until doubled in bulk, about 1½ hours.

7. Punch down, turn out onto floured board, and knead for a few minutes. Cut into 3 pieces. Shape each into a round cake, make a hole in the center, and stretch the dough out, forming a loop about 6 inches in diameter.

8. Place the rings on a greased baking sheet, cover, and let rise until doubled in size. Bake in 350° F oven for 20 to 25 minutes, or until golden brown.

9. Place on wire rack. If desired, spread Orange Glaze over warm loaf; cool completely.

Makes 3 8-inch rings.

Orange Glaze.

Sift 1 cup powdered sugar into a small bowl. Stir in ½ teaspoon grated orange rind and 2 tablespoons orange juice.

Italian Herb-Seasoned Breadcrumbs (Pane Grattagiatto)

Every cook suffers pangs of guilt when wasting food—particularly the "unusable" odds and ends of bread loaves, which accumulate with alarming regularity. Italian cooks put this bread surplus to good use by turning it into an herb-seasoned mixture that has a multitude of uses.

2 cups fine, dry breadcrumbs, preferably made from French bread
1 tablespoon finely minced parsley
½ cup finely chopped onion
¼ cup freshly grated Parmesan cheese
¼ teaspoon garlic powder
1 teaspoon dried oregano
½ teaspoon dried basil
½ teaspoon salt
⅛ teaspoon freshly ground black pepper

Combine all ingredients and store in tightly covered jar in the refrigerator. Will keep up to two weeks.

Uses. Breading meat, fish, and poultry; as a stuffing mix; or as a topping for casserole dishes.

Italian Easter Bread (Pane di Pasqua)

This colorful Easter bread is a traditional favorite with young children.

- ¼ cup lukewarm water (105° to 115° F)
- 1 teaspoon plus ¼ cup sugar
- 1 package active dry yeast
- 1 cup scalded milk
- 1 teaspoon salt
- ⅓ cup soft butter or margarine
- 2 eggs, beaten
- 3½ to 4 cups unsifted all-purpose flour
- ¼ cup drained and chopped red maraschino cherries
- 5 tinted eggs (instructions follow recipe)
- Glaze (recipe follows)

1. Combine water, one teaspoon sugar, and yeast in a small bowl, let stand 5 minutes.

2. In large bowl, combine milk, salt, butter, eggs, and remaining ¼ cup sugar. Add about ½ the flour and beat until smooth. Stir in yeast and cherries.

3. Add flour gradually to form a very stiff dough. Turn dough onto a heavily floured board and knead until smooth. Place in greased bowl; cover and let rise in warm place until doubled in bulk.

4. Punch down dough and return to lightly floured board. Divide in half. Roll each piece into a 24-inch rope. Loosely twist the ropes together and form them into a ring on a greased baking sheet.

5. Pinch the ends together, then gently spread the braid apart in five spots to make a nesting place for each egg. Push the eggs down into the dough as far as possible, being very careful not to crack them.

6. Cover braid with a towel and let rise a second time until double in bulk. Bake in 350° F oven 35 minutes, or until nicely browned.

7. Remove from baking sheet and cool on rack for 10 minutes before glazing. Serve slightly warm or at room temperature.

Makes one braid.

Tinted Eggs

Eggs do not need to be hard-cooked before tinting, as they will become hard during the baking process. However, hard cooked eggs can be used if desired. Tint egg shells with food color according to directions on package.

Glaze

- 1 tablespoon soft butter
- 1 cup powdered sugar
- 2 tablespoons milk
- ¼ teaspoon vanilla extract

Combine all ingredients and beat until smooth. Drizzle over warm baked bread.

The Italian bread basket overflows with a variety of plain loaves and sweet or spicy baked goods.

Seasoned Flat Hearth Bread (Focaccia)

Traditionally, this bread was baked on a clay or stone slab buried in ashes on the hearth; but today's **focaccia** is made in the oven in the conventional way. Serve hot or room temperature as an **antipasto**, or as bread to accompany any portion of the meal. It's a satisfying and perfect picnic food. For a quick loaf, use a thawed 1-pound loaf of frozen bread dough, pat evenly to fit inside a greased pan, and proceed with step 5.

- 1 1-ounce cake of fresh yeast or 1 package active dry yeast
- 1 cup warm water (105° to 115° F)
- 3 tablespoons olive oil
- 2 teaspoons salt
- About 3 cups flour
- Seasoned topping (recipe suggestions follow)

1. Place yeast in large bowl of electric mixer and sprinkle with water. Stir and let stand to dissolve, about 5 minutes.

2. Add oil, salt, and 2 cups of the flour to the yeast. Mix and beat at medium speed until dough is elastic. Add about ½ cup more of the flour until dough is stiff.

3. Place dough on a floured, smooth surface and knead until smooth and elastic, adding as much remaining flour as necessary.

4. Shape into a ball and place in an oiled bowl, turning dough to coat all sides. Cover with a dampened cloth towel and let rise in a warm place until doubled in size, from 1 to 3 hours.

5. Punch down the dough and roll out to form a rectangle that will fit into a greased 11 x 15 inch shallow baking pan. Pat dough into pan evenly. With your fingers, make indentations about 1 inch apart all over the dough. Add the topping of your choice from suggestions that follow.

6. Bake at 450° F until golden brown, about 15 to 20 minutes. Cut into strips or squares and serve hot or at room temperature.

Makes 6 to 10 servings.

Bacon Topping (Focaccia di Ciccioli)

Crisply fry 8 slices of bacon, drain on paper towels, and crumble over dough. Drizzle lightly with olive oil. Add 1 teaspoon crumbled dried whole sage leaves **or** 6 fresh ones, chopped, if you wish.

Onion Topping (Focaccia di Cipolle)

Cook 2 thinly sliced onions slowly in 3 tablespoons olive oil until soft, but not brown. Evenly spread onions and the pan drippings over the dough. Sprinkle with coarse salt.

Pizza Topping (Focaccia alla Pizzaiola)

Lightly brush dough with olive oil and pour over it ½ cup commercially prepared pizza sauce. Sprinkle with ½ cup freshly grated Parmesan, **romano**, or other dry cheese **or** shredded **mozzarella**. Drizzle with olive oil.

Sage Topping (Focaccia con la Salvia)

Sprinkle dough with about 1 dozen fresh sage leaves, chopped **or** 6 dried whole sage leaves, crumbled. Drizzle with olive oil and sprinkle with coarse salt.

Tomato Topping (Focaccia alla Pomodoro)

Lightly brush dough with olive oil and spread with 1 cup Basic Tomato Sauce (page 36) to which is added 2 cloves garlic, minced **or** your own favorite version. Sprinkle with chopped fresh basil to taste **or** 1 teaspoon crumbled dried basil **or** oregano. Evenly distribute 1 cup freshly grated Parmesan, **asiago**, or other dry cheese. Drizzle with olive oil.

Pizza Neapolitan Style (Pizza Napolitana)

Contrary to propaganda, pizza is not an American invention, but originated in Naples. It is an Italian art as old as bread baking, and every region of Italy has its own variation.

In the past, pizza was baked in communal adobe ovens, but today, brick or adobe oven baking is dying out even in Italy. Even in our modern ovens, however, the magical flavor and crisp texture created by brick ovens can be captured if you use a baking stone. To use, preheat the oven to 450° F and place the stone on the top rack at least 30 minutes before the pizza is ready to go in. If you don't have a baking stone, you may substitute quarry tiles, butted together in the oven. If you do not have either stone or tiles, bake pizza on a flat baking sheet. (Never use a pizza pan with a lip, it traps grease and ruins the crust.)

Following is the classic version of the pizza of Naples, followed by a few other topping suggestions. For variety, you can cut the risen dough ball into two or four pieces and roll out each one for individual pizzas.

Pizza Dough

- **½ ounce cake of fresh yeast** or **½ package dry yeast**
- **½ cup warm water**
- **1½ cups unbleached flour** or **imported** semolina **flour**
- **½ teaspoon salt**
- **1 teaspoon olive oil**

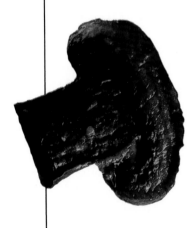

Pizza Filling

- **1½ cups chopped canned Italian-style plum tomatoes well-drained** or **1 pound fresh ripe plum tomatoes, peeled, chopped, and slightly cooked in olive oil to soften, then drained.**
- **½ pound mozzarella cheese, shredded**
- **6 flat anchovy filets, cut into small pieces**
- **1 teaspoon crumbled dried oregano** or **1 tablespoon chopped fresh oregano**
  Salt and freshly ground black pepper to taste

1. Dissolve yeast in warm water.

2. Place flour and salt in food processor bowl with steel knife. Slowly add yeast, then olive oil, and process until dough forms into one or more balls. Remove dough and knead by hand for 5 minutes. Or, to make by hand, place flour in a mound on a clean smooth surface and make a well in the center. Add remaining ingredients in the well. Gather flour from sides with a fork or fingertips. Working with your hands, combine into a dough ball, then knead until soft and smooth, adding flour as necessary until texture is satiny, about 10 to 15 minutes.

3. Place dough in a large oiled bowl and turn to coat with oil. Cover with a damp towel or plastic wrap and place in a warm spot until doubled in size, about 2 hours.

4. Punch dough down and turn onto a floured smooth surface. Flatten and roll out to a 10- or 11-inch diameter circle about ¼-inch thick, turning dough over occasionally as you roll. With fingertips, push dough toward edges, pinching up to make a rolled edge about twice as thick as the rest of the crust.

5. If the pizza will be cooked on a hot baking stone, place the dough on a floured wooden paddle or piece of heavy cardboard. Otherwise, place on a lightly floured baking sheet.

6. Just before you are ready to bake the pizza, lightly brush the dough with olive oil. Distribute tomatoes over the surface and sprinkle with the cheese. Add the anchovies, oregano, and seasonings.

7. Place the backing sheet in a hot 450° F oven. Or slide the pizza from the paddle or cardboard onto the hot stone. Bake until crust is golden and crisp and the cheese has melted, about 15 to 20 minutes. Serve piping hot.

Makes 2 to 4 servings

Variation. Omit anchovies and top with ¼ cup freshly grated Parmesan cheese before baking.

Pizza with Garlic and Tomatoes (Pizza alla Marinara)

Pizza dough (page 73)
1 tablespoon plus 3 tablespoons olive oil
1½ cups chopped canned Italian-style plum tomatoes well drained or 1 pound fresh tomatoes, peeled, chopped, and slightly cooked in olive oil to soften, then drained
2 cloves garlic, minced
Salt and freshly ground black pepper to taste
2 tablespoons chopped fresh oregano or 2 teaspoons crumbled dried oregano

1. Brush dough with olive oil and spread with tomatoes and garlic. Sprinkle with salt and pepper to taste. Top with oregano and drizzle with 3 tablespoons olive oil.

2. Bake in preheated 450°F oven as described in Step 7 of Pizza Neopolitan Style (page 73).

Pizza with Mushrooms (Pizza ai Funghi)

Pizza dough (page 73)
1 teaspoon olive oil
1½ cups chopped canned Italian-style plum tomatoes well drained or 1 pound fresh tomatoes, peeled, chopped, and slightly cooked in olive oil to soften, then drained
1 pound fresh mushrooms, sliced thinly
½ pound mozzarella cheese, shredded
Salt and freshly ground black pepper to taste
Olive oil

1. Brush dough with olive oil and add tomatoes and mozzarella cheese.

2. Cover top with mushrooms, add salt and pepper to taste, and lightly drizzle with olive oil.

3. Bake in preheated 450°F oven as described in Step 7 of Pizza Neopolitan Style (page 73).

Pizza with Mozzarella and Prosciutto (Pizza al Prosciutto)

Pizza dough (page 73)
1 teaspoon olive oil
⅓ cup prosciutto, cut into bite-sized pieces
½ pound mozzarella cheese, shredded
Olive oil

1. Brush dough with 1 teaspoon olive oil and spread with prosciutto. Drizzle on olive oil; add mozzarella.

2. Bake in preheated 450°F oven as described in Step 7 of Pizza Neopolitan Style (page 73).

Filled Pizza Turnovers (Calzone)

In this unusual version of pizza, an Italian sausage and tomato filling is encased in a crusty turnover.

Dough

1 package active dry yeast
1 cup warm water (105° to 115° F)
2½ to 3 cups sifted all-purpose flour
1 tablespoon sugar
1 teaspoon salt
1 tablespoon oil

1. In a large bowl, sprinkle yeast over warm water and let dissolve for 5 minutes.

2. Stir in 1 cup of flour, sugar, salt, and oil. Beat for 3 minutes. Continue adding flour ½ cup at a time, beating well after each addition, until a stiff dough is formed. This will take approximately another 1½ cups of flour.

3. Turn dough onto lightly floured surface; knead until smooth and elastic, incorporating more flour if necessary, about 10 minutes. Place dough in a greased bowl, turning to grease all sides. Cover, let rise in a warm place until doubled in size, about 1 hour.

4. Prepare filling.

Calzone Filling

½ pound sweet Italian sausage
1 small onion, sliced
¼ pound mushrooms, sliced
¾ cup diced green peppers
1 clove garlic, crushed
1 cup Basic Tomato Sauce (page 36) or canned tomato sauce
1 teaspoon dried oregano
½ teaspoon dried basil
½ teaspoon sugar
¼ teaspoon crushed red pepper
6 ounces mozzarella cheese, shredded
⅓ cup freshly grated Parmesan cheese

1. Prick casings of sausage and place in a cold skillet. Cover with water and place over medium heat. Cook for 10 minutes. Remove meat from casings and crumble into large chunks. Reserve 2 tablespoons of drippings.

2. In same skillet, combine drippings with sausage meat, onion, mushrooms, green pepper, and garlic; cook until tender. Stir in tomato sauce, herbs, sugar, and red pepper; simmer, uncovered, about 5 minutes. Let cool, then stir in mozzarella and Parmesan cheeses.

3. Punch down dough; divide into 10 equal pieces and form into flat balls. On a lightly floured surface, roll each ball into a 6-inch diameter circle.

4. On one side of circle, spoon approximately ⅓ cup of the filling. Fold plain half over filling, pinching edges together to seal.

5. Place on greased baking sheets and press edges together with tines of a fork. Prick tops with a fork and brush lightly with oil. Bake at 425° F for 15 minutes or until golden brown. Serve immediately.

Makes 10 turnovers.

Note. Baked calzone can be frozen. To serve, thaw completely, then bake at 350° F for 15 minutes.

Fried Cheese Turnovers (Panzaretti di Mozzarella)

These messy delights are a popular midday fare. Variations are served all over Italy.

Dough

6 cups flour
1½ teaspoons salt
6 tablespoons shortening
3 egg yolks
Milk

Filling

¾ pound mozzarella cheese, chopped and soaked in 3 tablespoons olive oil for 1 hour
1½ cups ricotta cheese, drained
1½ cups freshly grated Parmesan cheese
¼ pound prosciutto or ham, slivered
3 eggs, beaten
1 cup seeded, chopped, and well drained fresh or canned Italian-style plum tomatoes
¼ cup chopped parsley
Salt and freshly ground black pepper to taste
Oil and lard for deep frying (half-and-half is traditional, though you may use all oil)

1. Combine flour and salt in bowl and cut in shortening. Add egg yolks and mix well, adding a little milk, as needed, to make a fine, pliable dough. Knead until smooth and elastic. Cover dough and let rest for 30 minutes.

2. Combine cheeses, pork, eggs, tomatoes, parsley, salt, and pepper. Mix thoroughly.

3. Roll pastry very thin and cut into 5-inch rounds. Spoon filling into center, bring edges up and press together to form ball, sealing tightly.

4. Fry in hot oil, a few at a time, until golden brown, about 6 minutes. Remove with slotted spoon and drain on paper towel briefly. Serve piping hot wrapped in a waxed paper cone.

Makes about 12.

To dress garden-fresh salad in the bowl, pour over just enough good-quality olive oil to coat the greens but not enough to collect in the bottom. Toss thoroughly and follow with vinegar or lemon juice to taste, along with fresh or dried herbs, if you wish.

Salads (Insalata)

An Italian salad is served after the second course, and is designed to refresh the palate with garden-crisp greens and seasonal vegetables, cooked or raw. It is tossed with a simple dressing.

Compositions of meats, fish, fowl, rice, and pastas—such as Squid Marinade (page 24), Cold Spaghetti Salad (page 78), and Rice Salad (page 23)—are also called salads; however, these are served as *antipasti* or warm-weather first courses.

ITALIAN SALAD DRESSING

A good dressing for Italian salad should be understated and uncomplicated. Basic ingredients include salt, freshly ground pepper, olive oil (never substitute vegetable oil in a real Italian salad), wine vinegar or fresh lemon juice, and if you wish, fresh or dried herbs.

Always wash greens and vegetables and dry very well in a salad spinner, wire shaker basket, or towel before adding dressing. If the greens are still wet, the moisture will dilute the dressing ingredients and the oil will not properly coat the vegetables.

Standard proportions are 3 parts olive oil to 1 part vinegar or lemon juice. Adjust to your taste. Ingredients may be blended with a fork in a small bowl and poured over the salad **or** the ingredients may be individually added to the salad and tossed together.

If you choose to do it in this way, first lightly salt and pepper the salad. Then add enough olive oil to coat the vegetables, but not enough to collect in the bowl. Add only enough vinegar or lemon juice to create tartness, but not enough to overwhelm the other flavors. Then sprinkle on minced fresh or crumbled dried basil, parsley, or oregano, if you wish. Garlic may be rubbed into the salad bowl before adding any ingredients, **or** it may be pressed and steeped in the olive oil for a few minutes, then removed before oil is poured **or** rubbed into a piece of bread which is then tossed with the salad.

Toss gently but thoroughly to distribute dressing evenly. Taste and correct seasonings and serve immediately. Be sure not to let the salad sit long once it's dressed or it will become soggy. The entire procedure may be done at the table to ensure a crisp salad.

Mixed Salad (Insalata Mista)

Mixed salad is your chance to be creative. Use the following ingredients as a guide, and select fresh vegetables of your own choosing. Remember not to toss the whole garden into a bowl.

½ **head butter or other tender lettuce**
½ **head romaine lettuce**
½ **head curly chicory or escarole**
½ **bunch** arugola **(lamb's tongue)**
Garlic
½ **red or green sweet pepper**
1 **stalk celery**
1 **sweet fennel bulb**
1 **carrot**
4 **green onions** or ½ **sweet red onion, thinly sliced**
Fresh basil, chopped
Fresh parsley, chopped
1 **large tomato, diced**
Salt and freshly ground black pepper to taste
Olive oil
Red wine vinegar

1. Discard outer or damaged leaves from greens. Wash quickly and thoroughly in cold water and dry in a spinning basket or with a paper towel. Tear (don't chop) into bite-sized pieces in a large bowl that has been rubbed with cut garlic.

2. Wash pepper, remove seeds, and cut into bite-sized pieces, and toss into salad bowl.

3. Wash celery and fennel, trim away leaves, cut into thin crosswise slices, and add to greens.

4. Peel carrot, shred coarsely, and add to salad. Add sliced onions, herbs, and tomato.

5. Salt and pepper to taste, then add enough oil to coat ingredients. Sprinkle with a little vinegar and toss gently to mix well. Serve immediately.

Makes 6 servings.

Green Bean Salad (Fagiolini all' Oglio)

This method can also be used to prepare salads of cooked broccoli, cauliflower, or other mixed cooked vegetables.

1½ **pounds green beans, trimmed and washed**
Salt and freshly ground black pepper
Olive oil
Lemon juice

1. Boil beans, uncovered, in salted water until just tender but crisp to the bite. (Taste after 5 minutes; they may take up to 15 minutes depending on size and age.) Drain, and place beans in a shallow bowl.

2. Salt and pepper beans according to taste. Drizzle on olive oil to lightly coat beans, then add lemon juice to taste—dressing should be on the tart side. Toss and serve at room temperature, or chilled.

Makes 6 servings.

Note. Frozen green beans, preferably French-cut, and just barely cooked, can be used when fresh beans are not available.

Tossed Green Salad (Insalata Verde)

Select one, two, or three types of fresh greens—romaine, butter, Boston, and Australian lettuces; spinach, endive, curly chicory, escarole, watercress, sorrel, dandelion greens, and so on.

Trim wilted or damaged leaves and wash quickly but thoroughly. Dry in a spinning basket or towel.

Tear leaves into bite-sized pieces in a roomy salad bowl that has been rubbed with freshly cut garlic. Dress according to directions on page 75.

Variation. Add crumbled Gorgonzola or freshly grated Parmesan cheese.

Tomato Salad (Insalata di Pomodoro)

A delightful follow-up to first and second courses that are not prepared with tomatoes. The tomatoes used must be garden fresh.

4 to 5 **ripe tomatoes, peeled (if desired), and sliced**
Salt and freshly ground black pepper to taste
2 **tablespoons minced fresh basil** or 2 **teaspoons crumbled dried basil**
3 to 4 **tablespoons olive oil**
2 **tablespoons lemon juice** or **wine vinegar**

1. Arrange tomato slices with edges slightly overlapping on a platter. Add salt and pepper to taste, then sprinkle with basil. Drizzle with olive oil and lemon juice or vinegar. Let stand at room temperature about 30 minutes before serving, basting several times with dressing spooned from the platter.

Makes 6 to 8 servings.

Roasted Pepper and Mushroom Salad (Peperoni Arrosti e Funghi all' Oglio)

Savory, flavorful, and a pleasant change of pace from green salads.

5 or 6 **red or green sweet peppers**
4 **large, firm tomatoes**
1 **onion, cut into ½-inch chunks**
¼ **pound fresh mushrooms, cut into ¼-inch slices**
3 **tablespoons finely chopped parsley**
Marinade (recipe follows)
Sliced avocado or **hard-cooked eggs** or **tuna for garnish (all optional)**

1. To roast peppers, lay whole peppers on a foil-covered baking sheet. Bake at 350° F for 30 minutes or more, turning frequently as they begin to blister and brown. When done, put immediately into a brown paper bag and twist tightly closed. Allow to steam until cool, about 15 to 30 minutes. Skin will peel off very easily. Remove seeds and slice into bite-sized strips.

2. Peel tomatoes, halve, and discard seeds. Cut into wedges.

3. Steam onion lightly for 2 minutes, or until lightly softened but still a bit crisp.

4. Place peppers, tomatoes, onions, and sliced mushrooms in a 2-quart bowl and add parsley. Pour Marinade over the vegetables and mix well. To allow flavors to blend, let salad stand at room temperature for 4 hours before refrigerating. Garnish as desired. Serve chilled or at room temperature.

Makes 6 servings.

Marinade

In a small jar with lid, combine 5 tablespoons olive oil, 3 tablespoons red wine vinegar or lemon juice, 2 or 3 cloves garlic, pressed or minced, ½ teaspoon dried oregano, crushed, 2 tablespoons capers (optional), 1 teaspoon salt, and vinegar or lemon juice. Add capers and 1 teaspoon salt. Shake vigorously.

Variation. The following vegetables may be substituted for mushrooms or added for variety: ½ pound asparagus, lightly steamed and cut into chunks; 1 large raw zucchini, cut into ¼-inch thick slices; ¾ cup steamed corn; 1 cup eggplant chunks, lightly sautéed.

Colorful Roasted Pepper and Mushroom Salad is guaranteed to perk up any meal, both visually and to the taste. Try a garnish of sliced avocado with strips of roasted red pepper.

Among the most elegant of Italian salads is this one of asparagus coated in fruity green olive oil and white wine vinegar. It's traditionally served at room temperature, never chilled.

Asparagus Salad (Insalata di Asparagi)

There's no better way to enjoy tender young asparagus from the garden. Terrific picnic fare.

- **2 pounds fresh asparagus**
  Salt and freshly ground black pepper to taste
- **¼ cup olive oil**
- **1 tablespoon white wine vinegar**

1. Break off tough bottom end of asparagus and peel up several inches from the bottom with sharp knife or vegetable peeler. Cook in boiling salted water in an asparagus cooker or skillet (or your own favorite method) until tender but still firm to the bite. Remove from water and place to drain in a colander for about 25 minutes.

2. Arrange on a platter or in a shallow bowl. Add seasonings to taste, then cover with oil and vinegar. Serve at room temperature.

Makes 6 servings.

Potato and String Bean Salad (Insalata di Patate e Fagiolini)

A cold salad that can be prepared well in advance and goes with any meat or fish dish.

- **1 pound string beans, ends removed and cut in half**
- **4 large potatoes, peeled and cubed**
  Boiling salted water
- **¼ cup olive oil**
- **1 tablespoon wine vinegar**
- **½ teaspoon dried oregano**
  Salt and freshly ground black pepper to taste.

1. Cook string beans and potatoes separately in boiling salted water until beans are tender (about 30 minutes) and potatoes are cooked through, but still firm (about 20 minutes). Drain and combine in a serving bowl. Set aside to cool.

2. Combine olive oil, vinegar, and oregano. Pour over vegetables and season with salt and pepper to taste. Toss gently and refrigerate until serving time.

Makes 4 large servings.

Chilled Spaghetti Salad (Spaghetti alla Giudea)

A great picnic food.

- **1 pound spaghetti** or spaghettini
- **¼ cup plus 1 tablespoon olive oil**
- **1 cup peeled and thinly sliced sweet red pepper**
- **12 black olives, pitted and sliced**
- **3 tablespoons capers** or **½ cup cooked green peas**
- **1 2-ounce can anchovy filets, coarsely chopped**
- **2 tablespoons minced parsley**
  Juice of 1 lemon
  Salt and freshly ground pepper to taste

1. Cook pasta **al dente**, as directed on page 30, drain, and toss immediately with ¼ cup olive oil. Cool.

2. Toss with other ingredients and refrigerate at least 1 hour before serving or before leaving for picnic. Just before serving time, toss with 1 tablespoon olive oil and correct the seasonings.

Makes about 6 servings.

Variations. Try tiny bay shrimp or other cold cooked seafood tidbits in place of the anchovies. Or add minced hot pepper for a zesty taste. For a creamy salad, mix with a little homemade **Maionese** (page 21).

Fennel Salad (Insalata di Finocchio)

Bulbous, anise-flavored sweet fennel is served in Italy as a salad with just a coating of olive oil and plenty of pepper and salt.

- **1 sweet fennel bulb**
  Salt and freshly ground black pepper to taste
  Olive oil

1. Remove damaged outside stalks from fennel, discard a slice from the base of the bulb, and thinly slice the remainder horizontally. Wash slices in cold water and dry in a towel.

2. Place fennel in a bowl, add seasonings to taste, and generously coat with olive oil. Serve at room temperature.

Makes 4 servings.

Cheese (Formaggio)

Cheese is served after the salad course. A slice or wedge of just one cheese may be served on individual plates, or an assortment of Italian cheeses may be presented on a platter. Crusty Italian or French bread usually accompanies the cheese course, which is offered at midday and evening meals.

Serve cheese and bread alone if you plan on a sweet dessert to follow, or add fresh apples, pears, peaches, grapes, or other fruit if this is the meal's finale. For many Italians, there is no better climax to a great meal than pungent Gorgonzola spread on a juicy pear slice.

Cheese should be eaten at room temperature. Remove it from the refrigerator about an hour before serving time, leaving it covered to prevent drying of the cut surfaces. If you wish to arrange a cheese assortment several hours before serving, cover the presentation with plastic wrap to prevent drying until time for the cheese course.

STORING AND GRATING CHEESES

Cheeses require proper storage to prolong life and preserve freshness. Divide purchases into small pieces and wrap tightly in plastic wrap or foil to force out air. Then place the wrapped pieces in a plastic bag or airtight container and seal tightly. Keep bags or containers of cheese on the bottom shelf of refrigerator. Most hard cheese will keep for several months; soft cheeses should be used within a week. Trim away any mold that develops, except for edible mold that occurs on Gorgonzola.

Ricotta should be tightly covered and can be refrigerated for up to 5 or 6 days.

Small pieces of cheese to be used for cooking or crumbling into salads freeze well. Cut into serving-sized pieces, wrap tightly, and freeze. Thaw in the refrigerator one or two days before serving. (This takes planning ahead.)

The food processor or electric blender is the easiest way to grate cheese for cooking. For cheese that is to be sprinkled over pasta or into soup, a stainless steel hand-cranked grater, a grater-topped box, or the old four-sided model creates a better texture.

A quantity of grated Parmesan may be stored in the freezer in a tightly covered container. There is no need to thaw before using; cheese will melt as soon as it comes in contact with hot sauce.

Cheese in Olive Oil (Formaggio alla Olio d'Oliva)

Italian gourmets consider cheeses served in olive oil a special treat. Tangy **provolone**, soft **mozzarella**, or smoked **provola affumicate** are sliced thinly, placed in a shallow dish, drizzled with olive oil, and generously topped with freshly ground black pepper. **Taleggio**, **fontina**, or other soft cheeses can be mashed through a food mill, collected in a bowl, and covered with olive oil. Let stand overnight and serve at room temperature.

Cheese and Butter Mold (Cassatta di Formaggio)

Prepare this cheese mold a couple of days prior to serving and wrap tightly in plastic wrapping. A great dessert when accompanied by juicy fresh pears.

- **1 pound Gorgonzola, at room temperature**
- **1 pound sweet butter, at room temperature**
- **1 pound cream cheese, at room temperature**
- **¼ cup Cognac**
- **1 cup finely chopped walnuts**

1. Place Gorgonzola in food processor or mixer and blend until smooth. Reserve.

2. Prepare butter in same manner.

3. In a 4-cup mold, press the Gorgonzola and sweet butter in several alternating layers. Chill overnight.

4. Blend cream cheese with cognac until smooth and fluffy. Dip cheese mold into hot water for a few seconds and invert on a plate.

5. Frost with cream cheese and garnish wtih chopped walnuts. Serve with crusty bread or crackers.

Makes 8 to 12 servings

When pears are ripe and juicy, there's no better ending to the Italian meal than pear slices generously spread with tangy, blue-veined Gorgonzola cheese, often described as the "king" of table cheeses.

Fruit and Desserts (Frutta e Dolci)

Holidays and other special occasions mean that pastries and other rich desserts will be found at the Italian table. Ordinarily, however, the meal ends with fresh fruit or a simple dessert made from fruit.

Fresh Figs with Cream (Fichi alla Panna)

Peel ripe green or dark figs and cut in half. Soak in 1 or more ounces of Kirsch for about 1 hour. Arrange several halves on a dessert plate, and drizzle with fresh cream sweetened to taste.

Mixed Fruit Compote (Macedonia)

Macedonia is one of Italy's most popular desserts. It almost never contains the same combination of fruits twice.

2 cups freshly squeezed orange juice
Juice of 1 lemon or **lime**
1 lemon peel, grated (without white pith)
About 2 to 3 pounds of assorted fresh fruit—apricots, apples, canteloupes, honeydew melons, pears, bananas, plums, peaches, nectarines, grapes, mangos, papayas, and so on
About ½ cup sugar, more or less to taste and according to sweetness of fruit available
Orange or **cherry** or **anise liqueur**

1. Pour juices and lemon peel into a large bowl.
2. Wash fruit, peel, and core or pit. Grapes should be halved and seeds removed.

Cut all fruits into bite-sized pieces and combine with fruit juices, coating well to avoid darkening.

3. Add sugar to taste (you may wish to omit sugar completely), and liqueur. Cover and refrigerate several hours or even overnight, stirring several times to blend well.

Makes 6 to 8 servings.

Note. Should you wish to add strawberries, raspberries, blackberries, or other berries, do so at the last minute. This will prevent the berries from becoming soggy, and the other fruits from being stained by the berries. Bananas should also be last minute additions to prevent them from becoming brown and musty.

Poached Pears with Wine Custard (Pere allo Zabaglione)

Components of this elegant-looking dessert can be prepared a day or two ahead and assembled at the last minute.

Juice of 2 lemons
1 cup water
6 ripe but firm pears
½ cup sugar
2 cups white wine
1 cinnamon stick
3 strips of lemon peel
4 whole cloves
Cold wine custard or **Zabaglione (page 91)**
Crystalized violets (optional)

1. Combine lemon juice and water in a bowl.
2. Peel pears, leaving stems intact. Cut a slice off bottom of each pear to allow it to stand securely, and put pears into lemon juice and

water mixture to prevent discoloration.

3. Combine sugar, wine, cinnamon, lemon peel, and cloves in saucepan and bring to a boil. Add pears and poach until tender, about 30 to 45 minutes (depending on the ripeness of the pears). Let cool in poaching liquid, then chill.

4. Place pears on serving dish and spoon cold **Zabaglione** over top, letting it run down sides. Garnish with crystalized violets.

Makes 6 servings.

Peaches in Red Wine (Pesche al Vino)

Italians have been flavoring fruit with wine as far back as can be remembered. The wine is drunk with the meal; the fruit serves as dessert.

Allow one peach per person. Peel and pit each peach. Cut in halves, quarters, or slices. Place in a tall pitcher or individual wine glass and pour red wine over. Soak fruit for at least 30 minutes before serving. The longer the fruit is immersed, the better the wine.

Eat the peaches with a fork after the wine has been drunk.

Variations. Apples and oranges, alone or combined, can be substituted for the peaches when they are out of season. Dry white wine or champagne can be substituted for the red wine.

Baked Stuffed Peaches (Pesche al Forno)

Serve these hot, right out of the oven, or at room temperature. They can also be baked a day ahead and reheated.

6 large freestone peaches, ripe but firm
⅔ cup sugar
Grated rind of 1 lemon
2 egg yolks
¼ cup cocoa
8 or 10 almond macaroons (amaretti)
⅓ cup blanched almonds, finely chopped
Amaretto liqueur
2 to 3 tablespoons butter

1. Peel peaches, split, and remove stones. With a spoon, scoop out some of the pulp to leave a 1-inch shell.

2. In a bowl, combine scooped out peach pulp with ⅓ cup sugar, lemon rind, egg yolks, cocoa, crumbled cookies, and almonds. Add enough liqueur to form a thick paste.

3. Fill peach halves with stuffing mixture, arrange on a greased shallow baking dish, dot with butter, and sprinkle with remaining sugar. Bake at 400° F until peaches are tender, but still hold their shape, about 10 to 15 minutes. Serve warm.

Makes 6 servings.

The filling for Baked Stuffed Peaches combines almond and chocolate. Serve with espresso for a delightful afternoon treat or dessert.

Fruit Tart (Crostata di Frutta)

Like so many things that look and taste French to us, the origins of this dish are definitely Italian. This lovely tart can highlight a special meal or afternoon tea.

Flaky Sweet Pastry (Pasta Frolla) **(recipe follows)**
Pasta Cream (Crema Pasticciera) **(recipe follows)**
3 **cups sliced fresh and/or canned fruit, well drained**
½ **cup apricot preserves** or **orange marmalade**
½ **teaspoon orange liqueur** or **extract**

1. Prepare pastry and line a 9-inch tart or pie pan. Place in refrigerator or freezer until thoroughly chilled. Bake at 375° F for 15 to 20 minutes; cool thoroughly.

2. Prepare pastry cream; cool. Spread on cooled crust in an even layer. Top with fruit in desired pattern. In saucepan, heat preserves or marmalade; stir in orange liqueur or extract. Brush on fruit. Serve at room temperature or chilled.

Makes 8 servings.

Flaky Sweet Pastry (Pasta Frolla)

1¼ **cups all-purpose flour**
6 **tablespoons frozen sweet butter**
2 **tablespoons frozen shortening**
⅛ **teaspoon salt**
¼ **cup sugar**

1. Place all ingredients in a food processor and process until well blended and the consistency of cornmeal.

Add ice water slowly, up to 3 tablespoons. The dough will begin to form a ball when enough water has been added. **(Or combine by hand.)**

2. Working quickly, roll out to ⅛-inch thickness and place in tart pan as directed in recipe.

Pastry Cream

3 **egg yolks**
½ **cup sugar**
½ **cup flour**
1 **teaspoon vanilla extract**
1¼ **cups milk**

1. In a saucepan, beat egg yolks with sugar. Add flour and vanilla extract; beat until smooth.

2. Heat milk and add a little at a time, keep beating while cooking over a low flame, until mixture thickens. Do not boil. Remove from heat, cool slightly, and use as directed in recipe.

Strawberry Shortcake (Torta di Fragole)

Any fresh, sweet strawberry will do, but if possible choose tiny wild strawberries, varieties of **Fragaria vesca**, or **fraises des bois**, the European strawberry.

2 **cups ripe strawberries, hulled and halved**
¼ **cup sugar**
Juice of 1 lemon
¼ **cup orange liqueur**
1 **Genoa Cake,** or **1 9-inch Sponge Cake (page 82)**
Vanilla Custard Cream (page 83) or **Cold Wine Custard (page 91)**
1 **cup heavy cream, whipped with ¼ cup sugar and 1 teaspoon vanilla extract**

1. Cover strawberries with sugar, lemon juice, and liqueur. Let stand about 1 hour, then drain, reserving juice.

2. Split cake layer in half horizontally. Sprinkle ½ of the strawberry juice over bottom half. Spread with ½ of the Vanilla Custard or Cold Wine Custard. Scatter with berries and top with second half of the cake.

3. Sprinkle cake with remaining juice, spread with rest of the Vanilla Custard or Cold Wine Custard, and cover with whipped cream. Top with strawberries.

Makes 6 servings.

Nut-Stuffed Figs (Fichi Ripieni Mandori)

Dried figs are a popular sweet treat with the Italians, particularly when they are stuffed with nuts and rolled in sugar. The following recipes are holiday favorites.

Version I

24 **dried whole figs**
1 **cup orange juice**
1 **tablespoon lemon peel, grated**
1 **tablespoon lemon juice**
3 **tablespoons sugar**
24 **pecan halves**
Granulated sugar

1. Remove stem end from figs. Combine orange juice, lemon peel, lemon juice, and sugar. Pour over figs in saucepan; heat to boiling. Simmer, covered, until fruit is tender, about 45 minutes. Drain well and cool.

2. Insert knife in stem end of each fig to form a pocket. Fill each pocket with a pecan half. Roll figs in sugar until coated. Let dry overnight.

Makes 24.

Version II

24 **dried figs**
24 **blanched almonds or walnut halves**
¼ **teaspoon anise seed**
1 **cup sugar**

1. Slit figs on one side; insert nut. Spread on greased baking sheet and bake at 300°F for 15 minutes or until heated through and golden in color.

2. In a blender or food processor, combine anise seed and granulated sugar, blend to a fine powder.

3. Remove figs from oven and let cool. Roll in sugar mixture and serve as a confection. Store in a covered container.

Makes 24.

Light Genoa Cake layers are split and filled with chilled Zabaglione *(page 91) and strawberries in this Italian classic.*

Genoa Cake (Genoise)

Even in Genoa, its place of origin, this delicately textured cake is known by its French name. Serve as is, sprinkled generously with powdered sugar, or split and spread with your favorite filling. Use this cake in recipes calling for a light sponge cake, such as **Zuppa Inglese** (page 83).

6 eggs
1 cup sugar
1 cup sifted cake flour
½ cup butter, melted and cooled
1 teaspoon vanilla

1. Combine eggs and sugar in a large bowl or the top of a double boiler. Beat with an electric mixer or wire wisk until blended. Set bowl over a saucepan containing a small amount of warm water. Water in pan should not touch the bottom of the bowl. Place the saucepan containing the bowl over **very low** heat for 5 to 10 minutes, or just long enough for the eggs to become lukewarm. It is not necessary to beat them while they are warming, but they should be stirred occasionally to prevent them from cooking on the bottom of the bowl.

2. When eggs are lukewarm to the touch and begin to look bright yellow in color, remove from heat. With an electric mixer, beat at high speed until they are about triple in volume (this will take 10 to 15 minutes). Scrape the sides of the bowl with a rubber spatula when necessary.

3. When mixture begins to look like whipped cream, start to fold in flour, a little at a time, sprinkled on top of the whipped eggs.

4. When all of the flour has been folded in, very gently fold in the melted butter and vanilla. Take care not to overmix.

5. Grease and lightly flour a 9-inch springform pan, or 2 8-inch layer cake pans. Pour batter into prepared pan or pans, and bake in 350°F oven for 25 to 30 minutes. Remove from oven and let cool on a wire rack for 15 minutes. Remove from pan onto rack to cool thoroughly. Makes 6 servings.

Spongecake (Pane di Spagna)

This light, moist cake can be eaten plain, or used as the basis for other desserts.

6 eggs, separated
1 tablespoon lemon juice
1 cup sugar
⅛ teaspoon cream of tarter
1 cup all-purpose flour, sifted
¼ teaspoon salt

1. Grease and flour the **bottom only** of a 9-inch round springform cake pan. Shake off any excess flour.

2. Separate eggs. Beat yolks with lemon juice until thick and lemon colored. Gradually beat in ¾ cup of the sugar. Beat until very thick and light in color.

3. In another bowl, beat egg whites and cream of tarter until stiff. Gradually beat in remaining ¼ cup sugar, 1 tablespoon at a time, and continue to beat until meringue holds stiff peaks.

4. Fold egg yolk mixture into egg whites.

5. Sift flour and salt together. Fold into egg mixture ⅓ at a time, folding in each part gently but thoroughly.

6. Pour mixture into prepared pan. Bake at 350°F for 35 minutes, or until cake tester inserted in center comes out clean. Remove from oven and invert pan to cool thoroughly.

Florentine Dome Cake (Zuccotto)

This spectacular dessert, said to have been named after the cupola of Brunelleschi's Duomo in Florence, is composed of liqueur-soaked cake filled with layers of whipped cream and chocolate. It can easily be prepared a day or two in advance and unmolded just before serving.

1 9-inch spongecake (Pan de Spagna)

Syrup
⅓ cup sugar
⅓ cup water
¼ cup light rum
1 tablespoon orange liqueur

Filling I
1 teaspoon unflavored gelatin
1 tablespoon cold water
2 tablespoons orange liqueur (same type as used in making syrup)
1 cup heavy cream
¼ cup powdered sugar
2 ounces semi-sweet chocolate, finely grated

Filling II
3 ounces semi-sweet chocolate melted in ¼ cup heavy cream
1 cup heavy cream, beaten until stiff
2 tablespoons light rum
¼ cup filberts or walnuts, toasted and chopped
Powdered sugar

1. Remove cooled cake from pan and cut into ½-inch-thick slices. Arrange very close together around sides of a 2½- to 3-quart round bowl. Trim edges to fit. Cut one slice in half and use to cover bottom of bowl, trimming corners to fit. Make sure cake covers entire bottom and sides of bowl. Fill in any gaps with extra pieces of cake.

2. To make syrup, combine sugar and water in saucepan. Cook over medium heat until sugar is dissolved. Let cool, then stir in rum and liqueur. Sprinkle 7 tablespoons of syrup over spongecake lining the bowl. Cover with plastic wrap and refrigerate while preparing filling.

3. To prepare Filling I, in a small cup, dissolve gelatin in cold water. Place cup in small pan with about 1 inch of hot water. Stir over low heat until gelatin is completely dissolved. Remove from heat, let cool slightly. Stir in orange liqueur.

4. Whip cream until stiff, then beat in gelatin mixture and powdered sugar. Fold in grated chocolate. Spoon into cake-lined bowl and smooth into an even layer. Cover with a layer of spongecake and sprinkle with 2 tablespoons of the remaining syrup.

5. To prepare Filling II, combine chocolate and ¼ cup heavy cream in a pan of hot water. Stir to blend and let cool. Fold into heavy cream together with rum and chopped nuts.

6. Spoon into bowl over cake and cream layers. Cover top of mold with remaining cake slices trimmed to fit (some cake may be left over). Sprinkle remaining syrup over top. Cover with plastic wrap and chill several hours or overnight.

7. Just before serving, run a spatula around edge of bowl. Place a serving platter on top and invert cake. Sprinkle with powdered sugar and cut into wedges to serve.

Makes 10 to 12 servings.

Sicilian Feast Cake (Cassata alla Siciliana)

In Sicily this luxurious cake is served at feasts of renewal—Christmas, Easter, and wedding celebrations.

1 poundcake, about 9 x 5 inches, made from your favorite recipe or purchased from a bakery
2 cups ricotta **cheese**
¼ cup heavy cream
¼ cup sugar
¼ cup Strega or **orange liqueur**
4 tablespoons chopped mixed candied fruits
3 ounces semi-sweet chocolate, chopped finely
Chocolate Frosting (recipe follows)
Whole toasted almonds (optional)

1. Slice crusts from poundcake and trim top to level. With a serrated knife, cut horizontally into ½-inch slices. Place one layer on cake platter.

2. Sieve **ricotta** into a bowl and beat until smooth. Add cream, sugar, and liqueur, beating constantly. Gently fold in candied fruit and chocolate pieces. Spread on cake layer.

3. Top with another slice of cake and spread with more **ricotta**, aligning sides and ends as you work. Continue using all layers of cake and filling, topping with cake layer. Press gently to make the cake compact, smoothing filling and sides with rubber spatula. Cover with plastic wrap and refrigerate for several hours or until filling is firm.

4. When the cake is thoroughly chilled, prepare Chocolate Frosting. Frost sides, ends, and top of cake using a metal spatula to smooth. Place remaining frosting in pastry tube and decorate in swirls. Garnish with almonds, if desired. Loosely wrap cake in waxed paper and refrigerate overnight before serving. **Cassata** will keep well in the refrigerator for 3 to 4 days.

Makes 10 servings.

Chocolate Frosting

12 ounces semi-sweet chocolate, chopped
¾ cup espresso or **strong black coffee**
1 cup sweet butter, cut into small pieces and chilled

Melt chocolate in hot coffee over low heat, stirring well. Remove from heat and add butter, one piece at a time, beating with each addition until melted. Continue beating until smooth. Chill until frosting reaches spreading consistency.

Rum Custard Cake or "English Soup" (Zuppa Inglese)

It's neither English nor soup, though some stories say that this cake was invented as a copy of the English trifle which is also composed of sponge cake and custard. Like soup, the dessert should be eaten with a spoon and is best made a day ahead of serving.

2 cups Vanilla Custard Cream (recipe follows)
1 Genoa Cake (page 82) or Spongecake (page 82) cut into ¼-inch-thick slices
½ cup mixed liqueurs (Cherry Heering, Drambuie, Strega or others)
2 tablespoons rum
2 ounces semi-sweet chocolate chips, melted
3 egg whites
Pinch of salt
6 tablespoons sugar

1. Prepare custard and spread a little on bottom of a deep casserole dish and line the dish with a layer of cake. Sprinkle cake with about ⅓ of the mixed liqueurs.

2. Cover cake with ⅓ of the vanilla custard. Add another layer of cake and sprinkle on more liqueur and the rum.

3. Mix the melted chocolate with ½ of the remaining custard and spread over the cake.

4. Add another cake layer, more liqueur, and top with remaining vanilla custard.

5. Beat egg whites and salt until stiff, then gradually beat in sugar until whites are glossy. Spread over top of custard and bake at 350° F until meringue is pale ivory (do not allow to brown). Refrigerate at least 3 hours and preferably overnight before serving.

Makes about 6 servings.

Vanilla Custard Cream

2 cups milk
½ cup sugar
¼ cup cornstarch
½ teaspoon salt
2 eggs, beaten
1 tablespoon butter
1½ teaspoons vanilla extract

1. Place milk in top part of a double boiler over boiling water. Mix sugar, cornstarch, and salt. Stir into milk. Cook, stirring constantly, until thick. Cover; cook for 10 minutes longer.

2. Add small amount of mixture to eggs, return to double boiler, and cook for 5 minutes. Add butter. Put in bowl and sprinkle a small amount of sugar over top to prevent skin from forming. Chill; add vanilla and stir.

Makes about 2½ cups.

Variations. Instead of adding melted chocolate, stir in ½ cup chopped mixed candied fruit into the middle custard layer. In lieu of adding meringue, top custard with chopped toasted almonds or sweetened whipped cream and garnish with pieces of candied fruit.

Note. 24 Ladyfingers, either homemade using recipe on page 91, or purchased, can be substituted for the Genoa Cake or Spongecake.

The pastries in Italian shops are irresistible.

Serve slightly sweet orange-flavored ricotta Cheese Pie for a morning coffee break or afternoon snack.

Cheese Pie (Crostata di Ricotta)

The not-too-sweet filling makes a delicious morning coffee break, brunch offering, or afternoon snack.

**Flaky Sweet Pastry
(page 81)**
Ricotta **Cheese Filling
(recipe follows)**

1. Prepare pastry; reserve ¼ of dough for trimmings. Carefully line a 9-inch removable-bottom cheesecake or regular pie pan with the remaining dough. Chill.

2. Prepare **Ricotta** Cheese Filling. Pour into pastry shell. Roll out reserved dough into a 12-inch rectangle. Cut into strips ½ inch wide with a sharp knife or pastry wheel. Crisscross strips on top to form lattice design.

3. Bake at 350° F for about 30 minutes, or until center of filling feels firm and crust is golden. Serve slightly warm. Pie may be reheated after refrigerator storage.

Makes 8 servings.

Ricotta Cheese Filling

- **4 cups** Ricotta **cheese** or **small-curd cottage cheese, pushed through a sieve**
- **1 egg yolk**
- **⅓ cup sugar**
- **¼ teaspoon salt**
- **2 tablespoons grated orange peel**
- **1 teaspoon vanilla extract**
- **1 tablespon Amaretto liqueur** or **Marsala wine**
- **3 egg whites**

1. Mix cheese, egg yolk, sugar, salt, grated orange peel, vanilla extract, and Amaretto liqueur or Marsala wine. Beat until smooth.

2. Fold in egg whites, beaten stiff but not dry, and pour into pastry shell.

Optional. Add one or more of the following to the **Ricotta** Cheese Filling mixture: 1 tablespoon raisins, diced candied citron, or diced candied lemon or orange peel; **or** 2 tablespoons slivered blanched almonds, pine nuts, or semi-sweet chocolate bits.

Sicilian Fried Stuffed Pastries (Cannoli)

Cylindrical **cannoli** or "pipes" have long been associated with fertility and rebirth, thus they're favored pastries at Italian weddings and Easter celebrations.

Dough

- 4 **cups sifted all-purpose flour**
- 2 **tablespoons sugar**
- 1/4 **teaspoon salt**
- 3 **tablespoons butter**
- 2 **egg yolks**
  Approximately 1/2 cup white wine
  Shortening or vegetable oil for deep frying
  Filling and Garnish (suggestions follow)

1. Mix flour, sugar, and salt in a bowl. Cut in butter, then add egg yolks. With a fork, stir in wine, 1 tablespoon at a time, until dough clings together. Form into a ball, cover, and let stand about 30 minutes.

2. Roll dough paper thin on floured board and cut 4-inch circles. Wrap circles around metal **cannoli** tubes, turning each end back to flare slightly. Fry a few at a time in deep fat until golden, about 1 minute. Remove with tongs and drain on paper towels. Carefully slip out tubes after about 5 seconds. Cool shells.

3. Before serving, force filling into **cannoli** shell through large pastry tube. Sift powdered sugar over pastry shell and garnish filled ends with chopped candied fruits, coarsely grated chocolate, or chopped nuts.

Makes about 24 pastries.

Note. Shells may be stored in airtight containers for several days prior to filling, or purchased ready-made from Italian markets. Just add fillings for quick desserts. In lieu of **cannoli** tubes, cut a 1-inch aluminum tubing from the hardware store into pieces about 4½ inches long.

Traditional Ricotta Filling

- 4 **cups** ricotta **cheese**
- 1½ **cups powdered sugar**
- 1 **tablespoon vanilla extract**
- 1/3 **cup finely chopped mixed candied fruits**
- 1/4 **cup coarsely chopped semi-sweet chocolate**
- 1 **cup heavy cream, whipped to form stiff peaks (optional)**

Press **ricotta** cheese through wire sieve or blend until smooth in food processor or blender. Mix with powderd sugar and vanilla extract. Add finely chopped mixed candied fruits and chocolate. Chill before using. For a lighter filling, fold in whipped cream.

Pistachio Cream Filling

Prepare **Ricotta** Filling and add a few drops of green food coloring. Stir in food coloring. Stir in chopped pistachio nuts instead of the mixed fruits and chocolate. Garnish ends with more pistachio nuts.

Whipped Cream Filling

Fill shells with sweetened whipped cream. Garnish ends with grated chocolate and candied whole cherries.

Orange Cream Filling

To sweetened whipped cream, add orange liqueur to taste and grated orange rind. Garnish ends with more grated orange rind.

Custard Filling

Fill **cannoli** with your favorite vanila custard cream. Garnish with chocolate bits or crushed Italian-roast coffee beans.

Pudding Filling

Fill **cannoli** with any flavor pudding mixture.

Puréed Chestnut with Whipped Cream (Monte Bianco)

One of the best of Italian classic desserts. It represents Monte Bianco, a snow-clad mountain in the Italian Alps. This dessert is best made a short time before serving.

- 2 **pounds chestnuts**
  Cold water
- 2 **cups milk**
- 3/4 **cup sugar**
- 1/2 **teaspoon vanilla extract**
  Pinch salt
- 2 **tablespoons rum**
- 1 **cup heavy cream**
- 2 **tablespoons powdered sugar**

1. With the point of a sharp knife, score the flat sides of the chestnuts with an "X." Place in pot, cover with cold water, bring to boiling, and simmer for 30 minutes. Drain and peel while still warm, removing only a few from the water at a time.

2. Combine milk, sugar, salt, and vanilla, and scald. Drop peeled chestnuts into the milk. Simmer, uncovered, over very low heat until tender but not mushy, about 15 to 20 minutes. Drain, reserving the milk for custard or other puddings.

3. Mash the chestnuts finely with a fork and stir in 1 tablespoon rum. Press the mixture through a colander or sieve with coarse holes (or press through a potato ricer) directly onto a serving plate. Allow mixture to fall freely into a cone-shaped mound. Do not try to shape in any way, the chestnuts must remain loose and fluffy.

4. Beat the heavy cream until it forms soft peaks, then stir in the remaining 1 tablespoon rum and powdered sugar. Lightly spoon mixture over the chestnut mound, letting it stream casually down the sides. Best served immediately, but may be refrigerated for no more than 1 hour.

Makes 6 to 8 servings.

Strong Plate (Piatto Forte)

A very old and complicated version of this recipe instructs that a plate be laid over the bowl and weighted down with heavy rocks or an iron. When the dessert was unmolded, it retained the shape of the bowl—thus the name **piatto forte**, or "strong plate." Both the ingredients and method have changed over the years, but the name remains.

- 4 **cups milk**
- 4 **tablespoons cornstarch**
- 4 **eggs, slightly beaten**
- 1 **cup sugar**
- 1/2 **teaspoon salt**
- 1 **teaspoon vanilla**
- 1/2 **cup mixed rum and brandy**
- 2 **dozen ladyfingers, purchased** or **made from** Savoiardi **recipe (page 91)**
- 1/2 **cup canned chocolate syrup**
  Maraschino cherries (optional)

1. Combine 1 cup of the milk and the cornstarch. When well blended add remaining 3 cups milk and set aside.

2. In the top of a double boiler, blend the beaten eggs, sugar, and salt. Slowly add the milk mixture. Place over hot, not boiling, water. Cook and stir until mixture thickens. Remove from heat and cool thoroughly. Add vanilla.

3. Place the rum and brandy in a shallow bowl. Very lightly dip the bottoms of the ladyfingers in the mixture and arrange a layer of them across the bottom of a deep 2-quart bowl. Pour 1/3 of the custard sauce over the ladyfingers and drizzle 1/3 of the chocolate syrup over the custard. Repeat layers two more times or until all ingredients have been used, ending with chocolate syrup.

4. Decorate with maraschino cherries, if desired. Cover with plastic wrap and refrigerate several hours or overnight before serving.

Makes 8 servings.

The Swans of Villa d' Este (I Cigni di Villa d' Este)

Graceful, delicate cream puff swans filled with rich, creamy **zabaglione** sauce will highlight your fanciest dinner. Your own favorite puff pastry recipe may be substituted.

Puff Pastry

2½ cups water
1 cup butter
1 vanilla bean, split (optional)
½ teaspoon salt
2½ cups flour
10 eggs
Zabaglione **Cream** (recipe follows)

1. In a large saucepan, heat water. Add butter, vanilla bean, and salt. When butter is melted, remove bean and save for another recipe. Stir in flour until batter forms a large mass and comes away from the sides of the pan. Remove from heat and cool.

2. Add eggs, one at a time, beating well after each addition until mixture is very smooth.

3. Place dough in a pastry bag. Squeeze heaping tablespoons 3 inches apart onto greased baking sheets. Repeat to make 12 to 15 shells. Try to form the dough into the shape of pears, as they will later become the swan's bodies.

4. On another baking sheet, with a small opening plain hole tube attached to the pastry bag, form an equal number of pieces shaped like the number 2. (These will be the heads and necks.)

5. Bake bodies in a preheated 400° F oven for 10 minutes. Reduce heat to 350° F and bake for about 25 minutes longer. Do not remove from oven until they are quite firm to the touch. Bake head and neck sections in preheated 400° F oven for only 10 minutes. Cool both parts thoroughly before filling.

6. Prepare the **Zabaglione** Cream and reserve.

7. Cut off the top portion of each swan body and reserve. Fill the lower portion with the **Zabaglione** Cream. Divide the top piece in half crosswise for the wings. Stick the necks upright into the cream at one end. Embed the wings somewhat diagonally into the filling on either side of the neck. Dust the whole swan lightly with powdered sugar, if desired.
Makes 12 to 15 servings.

Zabaglione Cream

¼ cup granulated sugar
1 tablespoon flour
⅛ teaspoon salt
5 egg yolks
½ cup Marsala wine
1 teaspoon vanilla extract
1 cup heavy cream
3 egg whites
¼ cup powdered sugar

1. Mix together in the top of a double boiler sugar, flour, and salt.

2. Beat egg yolks until thick and lemon colored. Stir into sugar mixture. Cook over hot water, stirring constantly until thick. Remove from heat and add Marsala and vanilla. Chill until cool but not set, stirring occasionally.

3. Whip heavy cream until stiff and fold into egg yolk mixture. Beat egg whites until foamy. Gradually add powdered sugar and beat until stiff. Fold egg whites into egg yolk mixture. Place in pastry bag and squeeze into puffs.

Note. Puffs for bodies and heads can be made ahead and refrigerated or frozen. Fill and assemble just prior to serving. Vanilla custard or whipped cream can be substituted for **Zabaglione** Cream.

Cream puff swans are an Italian tradition. This version comes from the Villa d'Este. The cream puffs are presented on blue-tinted gelatin to suggest the clear waters of Lake Como.

Italian Bread Pudding (Budino di Pane)

A fine soufflé-like pudding with a caramel glaze, this dessert shows no evidence that bread is the main ingredient. Best made a day or two in advance of serving—it improves in both texture and flavor as it rests.

Caramel Glaze

1 cup sugar
1 to 2 tablespoons boiling water

1. In a heavy skillet, combine the sugar and 1 tablespoon of the boiling water. Beat over medium-high heat until sugar turns a very dark brown. Slowly add a little more boiling water until the sugar is completely dissolved and syrup becomes very thick. Watch carefully to prevent burning.

2. Pour syrup into an 8-inch round aluminum cake pan. Tip the pan in all directions so sides and bottom are completely covered with the thick syrup. If syrup hardens before pan is completely covered, return to heat momentarily. When entirely covered, refrigerate pan until syrup becomes cold and caramelized.

Pudding

8 slices firm white bread, crusts removed
¼ cup currants
½ cup butter
Juice of 1 lemon
⅓ cup ground almonds
1 cup milk
1 cup sweetened condensed milk
4 large eggs, beaten
2 teaspoons vanilla extract
2 teaspoons almond extract

1. Tear 2 slices of the bread into very small pieces and arrange on bottom of caramelized cake pan. Sprinkle 8 to 10 currants and ¼ each of the butter pieces, lemon juice, and ground almonds over the bread pieces. Repeat layers three more times, until all ingredients are used.

2. Combine milk, sweetened condensed milk, eggs, and vanilla and almond extracts. Beat until smooth and pour over the bread mixture. Allow a few minutes for the bread to absorb the liquid. If liquid does not come to the very top of the pan, add a little more milk. Let mixture set at room temperature for 1 hour.

3. Set the pudding mold in a large shallow baking dish. Add warm water to a depth of ½-inch around the sides of the mold. Bake in a 325° F oven for 1 hour. Immediately turn out upside down onto a serving plate.

Sauce

4 tablespoons bourbon or rum
3 tablespoons boiling water

Pour bourbon or rum and boiling water into the pudding mold and set over medium heat. Stir until pan is deglazed. Spoon sauce over pudding. Refrigerate for at least 24 hours prior to serving.

Makes 8 to 10 servings.

Ricotta Cheese with Coffee (Ricotta al Caffè)

Ricotta cheese is a very popular cooking ingredient all over Italy. Its versatility stretches all the way from savory dishes like lasagne to sweet desserts.

1 pound ricotta cheese
¾ cup powdered sugar
¼ cup freshly brewed strong black coffee
¼ cup dark rum
¼ cup finely chopped walnuts

1. In a food processor or blender, combine the ricotta cheese, sugar, coffee, and rum until mixture is smooth and thick. Refrigerate for at least 2 hours, or until thoroughly chilled.

2. Spoon the mixture into individual serving glasses or custard cups. Sprinkle chopped nuts over top.

Makes 4 to 6 servings.

Anise Biscuits (Biscotti al 'Ancice)

A favorite for dunking into wine or coffee, these twice-baked cookies are often called "anisette toast." They're long keepers when stored in airtight containers.

1 cup sugar
½ cup butter
3 eggs (reserve 1 yolk)
1 teaspoon anise extract
1 teaspoon anise seed
3 cups all-purpose flour
½ teaspoon salt
2 teaspoons baking powder
1 tablespoon milk
Multicolored sprinkles (optional)

1. Cream sugar and butter, add eggs (reserve 1 yolk), and beat well. Stir in anise extract and anise seed.

2. Combine flour, salt, and baking powder. Thoroughly blend into sugar and egg mixture.

3. On greased baking sheets, form dough into two long, flat loaves ½ inch thick by 2 inches wide. Combine reserved yolk and 1 tablespoon milk, brush over top of loaves. Sprinkle with multicolored sprinkles, if desired. Bake at 375° F for 20 minutes. Remove from oven and cool slightly.

4. Cut into 1-inch diagonal slices. Replace on baking sheets, cut side down, and return to oven. Bake for 5 minutes on each side, or until golden. After cooling on wire racks, store in airtight containers.

Makes about 3 dozen.

Fried Cookies (Cenci)

Puffed fried bows of pastry are a treat for everyone. They can be stored in airtight containers for up to 2 weeks, or frozen for longer keeping.

2 eggs
2 egg yolks
2 tablespoons heavy cream
1 teaspoon salt
1 tablespoon granulated sugar
2½ cups flour
Vegetable oil for deep frying
Powdered sugar

1. Beat whole eggs, yolks, cream, salt, sugar, and flour until well blended. The dough will be soft.

2. Turn onto well-floured board and knead lightly until coated in flour. Continue kneading until dough feels smooth, about 5 minutes. Cover and chill for 2 to 3 hours.

3. Cut into four equal pieces, then roll each piece until dough is paper thin. Cut with sharp knife or pastry wheel into ½ x 6 inch strips. Fold strips into a loop and thread one end through to form a loose knot; do not pull or dough will break.

4. Drop a few at a time into deep fat, about 375° F, and fry for 1 or 2 minutes on each side, or until golden. Drain on paper towels. Sprinkle with powdered sugar when cool.

Makes about 4 dozen.

Almond Balls (Pastini di Mandorla)

Butter cookies rolled in almonds then filled with jam are popular and easy to make.

½ **cup butter**
1 **cup sugar**
1 **egg**
1 **teaspoon sherry wine** or **almond extract**
2 **cups plus ¼ cup sifted all-purpose flour**
1 **teaspoon baking powder**
Pinch salt
2 **tablespoons milk**
1 **egg white, beaten**
1 **cup chopped almonds**
Apricot or **strawberry jam**

1. Cream butter, sugar, and egg. Add flavoring.

2. Blend 2 cups flour, baking powder, and salt together. Add to butter mixture alternately with milk. Mix well. Turn dough out on to lightly floured board and knead in remaining ¼ cup flour. Chill dough several hours or overnight.

3. Pinch off small pieces of dough about the size of a walnut. Shape into balls, drop into beaten egg white, then roll in chopped almonds.

4. Place on greased baking sheets. With thumb, make an indentation in the center of each cookie. Bake at 350°F for 10 minutes. Remove from oven; if indentation has risen press down again with back of a small teaspoon. Drop a small bit of jam into each indentation and return to oven for 2 to 3 minutes, or until cookies are lightly browned.

Makes about 3 dozen cookies.

Cannoli are fried Sicilian pastries that can be stuffed with an infinite variety of fillings. See page 85 for suggestions, or create your own variations.

Florentines

Half candy and half cookie, these cookies are rich and sweet, and excellent with coffee. Named after the city of Florence, they are said to date back to the fifteenth or sixteenth century.

¾ **cup sliced almonds**
¼ **cup heavy cream**
⅓ **cup sugar**
¼ **cup butter**
¼ **cup all-purpose flour**
½ **cup very finely chopped candied orange peel**
6 **ounces semi-sweet chocolate**
1 **teaspoon vegetable shortening**

1. Whirl ½ the almonds in a blender or food processor until fine.

2. In a saucepan over low heat, combine cream, sugar, and butter. Stir occasionally until butter is melted. Turn heat to medium-high, bring mixture to a boil, and remove from heat.

3. Stir in ground almonds and flour to make a thin batter. Stir in remaining sliced almonds and orange peel.

4. Drop by scant teaspoonfuls about 2 inches apart onto heavily greased and floured baking sheets. Flatten with the back of a spoon to about 1½ inches in diameter.

5. Bake at 350°F for 8 to 10 minutes, or until edges start to brown. Cool on pan 2 or 3 minutes or until cookies become firmer. Place on wire rack to cool thoroughly.

6. Combine chocolate and vegetable shortening in top of a double boiler over hot, not boiling water. Turn cookies over and brush chocolate coating on underside of each with a pastry brush. Let dry several hours until chocolate hardens. Store in covered container in refrigerator or freezer.

Makes 30 cookies.

Italian Pastry Puffs (Sfingi)

On March 19, Italians pay homage to St. Joseph, the patron saint of home and family. No St. Joseph's day would be without **sfingi**, large round puffs deep fried, filled with sweetened ricotta, and topped with a red cherry.

Puffs

½ **cup butter**
2 **tablespoons sugar**
1½ **cups boiling water**
1¼ **cups all-purpose flour**

4 **eggs**
Oil for deep frying
Maraschino cherry halves

Filling

1 **pound** ricotta **cheese**
½ **cup powdered sugar**
½ **teaspoon cinnamon**

¼ **cup finely minced candied fruit**

1. Add butter and sugar to boiling water and bring to boiling point. Add flour all at once, and stir vigorously until ball forms in center of pan, about 1 minute. Remove from heat and cool slightly.

2. Add eggs to mixture, one at a time, beating well after each addition.

3. Heat oil in a deep pot to 375°F. Slip batter from tablespoon into hot oil and fry puffs until golden in color. They will expand and turn themselves as they cook.

Remove with slotted spoon and drain on absorbent paper.

4. Combine all filling ingredients. Before serving, split puffs in half and fill. Dust with powdered sugar and top with a cherry.

Makes approximately 2 dozen.

Sesame Cookies (Biscotti di Giugliulena)

Italians are not big breakfast eaters. Usually, breakfast consists of steaming **espresso** laced with hot milk (**caffè latte**) and an assortment of pastries, breads, or cookies for dunking. This not-too-sweet cookie is a Sicilian favorite.

4 cups all-purpose flour, sifted
1 cup sugar
½ teaspoon salt
4 teaspoons baking powder
½ cup melted butter
3 eggs, blended
1½ teaspoons vanilla extract
½ cup sesame seeds

1. Sift flour, sugar, salt, and baking powder together into a large bowl. Make a well in the center. Into the well pour melted butter, eggs, and vanilla extract. Mix until the dough is smooth. Gather up with fingers and form into a ball. Cut ball into 4 pieces.

2. On a lightly floured board, roll pieces with palms of hands, forming long ropes, ½-inch thick. Cut ropes into 2-inch lengths. Brush each cookie with water and roll in sesame seeds, coating well.

3. Place cookies, 1 inch apart, on greased baking sheets. Bake in 350° F oven until cookies are browned, 12 to 15 minutes.

Makes about 6 dozen cookies.

Stovetop Cookies (Pizzelle)

Bake these thin wafers over a burner in either the **cialde** or **pizzelle** hinged cookie irons, or substitute one of the Scandinavian irons.

4 eggs
¾ cup sugar
½ cup vegetable oil
2 cups flour
½ teaspoon baking powder
Pinch salt
1 tablespoon vanilla extract
2 teaspoons grated orange peel

1. Combine all ingredients and beat together until batter is smooth.

2. Heat cookie iron over medium heat, turning occasionally, until hot enough to make a drop of water dance. Pour batter one tablespoon at a time into center. Close iron and cook, turning several times, until cookie is golden. Remove from iron and cool on wire rack. Repeat until batter is gone.

Makes about 24 cookies.

Variation. While still warm, roll the cookie into a cylinder. Fill with cold **zabaglione** or sweetened whipped cream.

Menu suggestions. Serve **pizzelle** with ice cream or a glass of wine.

When you're in the mood for baking or have a good Italian bakery nearby, stage an afternoon party featuring an assortment of cookies to be enjoyed with wine, as the Italians do, or with tea or coffee.

The perfect ending to an Italian meal is a bowl of seasonal fruits immersed in chilled (not iced) water, bubbly mineral water, or best yet, sparkling dessert wine. Everyone chooses fruits from the communal bowl, which doubled as a table decoration during the meal.

Fig Cookies (Cucidati)

This cookie is a traditional treat in Sicilian homes at Christmas time, but almost unknown outside of Sicily. The mother of one of our editors shared her version with us. Although it is time-consuming, it can be done in stages and is well worth the effort.

Filling

2 pieces candied citron	Peel of one fresh
12 pieces candied orange peel	tangerine
	3 pounds dried figs
3 pieces candied lemon peel	1/2 cup almonds
	1/2 cup walnuts
12 pieces candied pineapple	1/4 cup sherry wine
	1/4 cup brandy
3/4 pound dark raisins	1 ounce semi-sweet chocolate, grated
3/4 pound golden raisins	
1/2 pound candied cherries	1 teaspoon cinnamon
	1/4 teaspoon allspice
Peel of one fresh orange	1 10-ounce jar quince or plum jelly

Pastry

3 cups all-purpose flour, sifted	1/2 cup sugar
	3 eggs, beaten
1/2 teaspoon salt	1 1/2 teaspoons vanilla
1 1/2 teaspoons baking powder	
1/2 cup solid vegetable shortening	

1. Preheat oven to 375°F. Using a meat grinder with a medium blade, grind all the candied fruit, dried fruit, peel, and nuts together **twice**, or chop finely in a food processor. Stir in wine, brandy, chocolate, spices, and jelly. Add 2 tablespoons sherry, or more if mixture is too thick to blend evenly. Set aside.

2. To make pastry, sift flour, salt, and baking powder together. Cream shortening and sugar together, adding eggs and vanilla. Blend well, then gradually stir in flour mixture until a smooth dough forms. Gather up with fingers and form into a ball.

3. Turn onto a lightly floured board and roll out to 1/4-inch thick. Cut dough into 4-inch strips. Spread a row of filling 1 inch thick over one half of strip. Fold over other half to cover filling. With fingers or fork, press edges together to seal filling in. Using a very sharp knife, slice strip on a slant into 2-inch slices. Repeat process until all dough and filling are used.

4. Arrange slices 1 inch apart on greased baking sheets and bake until lightly browned, about 10 to 15 minutes. Do not overbake. Remove from oven and cool on wire racks. Glaze cookies with Icing and decorate with multicolored sprinkles.

Icing

1 1/2 cups powdered sugar	
Juice of 1 or 2 lemons	
Multicolored sprinkles	

Combine powdered sugar and lemon juice; mix into smooth glaze.

Note. These cookies will store well for up to 2 weeks in an airtight container, or for several months in the freezer. Both the filling and the dough can be made in advance and kept in the refrigerator for up to 1 week.

Fruit Ices (Granita di Frutta)

Fruit **granita** are puréed fruits sweetened with sugar syrup and frozen until gritty in texture. What could be simpler to prepare? Here is a basic recipe with citrus and coffee variations.

2 1/2 cups sugar, approximately (depending upon sweetness of fruit used)
1 3/4 cups water
5 cups peeled and pitted fresh fruit puréed in food processor, then pressed through a fine sieve. Suggested fruits: apricots, peaches, melons, blackberries, strawberries, raspberries, pears, figs, papaya, mango, and so on
Freshly squeezed juice of 1 lemon and 1 orange, strained

1. Over medium heat, cook sugar and water in heavy saucepan until syrup reaches thread stage or 219°F on candy thermometer.

2. Pour cooked syrup over fruit purée in a large bowl. Let cool to room temperature, then add lemon and orange juice. Chill in refrigerator.

3. Pour fruit mixture into ice trays that have been well washed with baking soda and water to remove any foreign odors or tastes, and then well rinsed. Place in refrigerator freezer unit that has been turned to coldest temperature. Freeze until almost solid.

4. Turn frozen mixture into a large bowl and chop thoroughly, or run briefly through food processor with steel knife. Return to ice trays and freezer until solid once again.

5. Repeat Step 4, then pour into chilled stemmed glasses or dessert dishes. Place in freezer until serving time.

Makes about 6 servings.

Note. You can create a finer-textured ice by adding 2 egg whites to the above mixture and freezing in an ice cream freezer.

Variations. Consider serving any of the fruit ices in hollowed shells of fruit such as papaya, mango, tangerines. Garnish with mint sprigs.

Lemon Ice (Granita di Limone)

Prepare sugar and water syrup as in Step 1 of Fruit Ice (preceding). Cool syrup, then mix with 2 cups freshly squeezed lemon juice, the grated rind of 2 lemons (without white bitter pith), and 1 cup cold water. Refrigerate until cold, then proceed with freezing as in Steps 4 and 5.
Makes about 4 servings.

Orange Ice (Granita di Arancia)

Follow recipe for Lemon Ice above, substituting orange juice and orange rind. Add the juice of 2 lemons.

Grapefruit Ice (Granita di Pompelmo)

Substitute grapefruit juice for the lemon juice in Lemon Ice above. Add grated rind of 1 lemon and 1 orange, and complete as for Lemon Ice.

Coffee Ice (Granita di Caffè)

Top with whipped cream, or make alternating layers of coffee ice and whipped cream in parfait or other stemmed glasses. A summer afternoon delight.

1¾ cups sugar
2 cups water
3 cups espresso **or dark French roast coffee**
Whipped cream for garnish

1. Prepare syrup of sugar and water as in Step 1 of Fruit Ice (page 90). Cool.
2. Add coffee, chill, and freeze as in Fruit Ice, Steps 4 and 5 (page 90). Garnish with whipped cream.

Spumone

The paper-lined wedge studded with tutti-frutti that Americans know as **Spumone** is far different from the real thing. This Sicilian specialty is accented with the flavor of blood oranges.

Vegetable oil
Grated rind of 1 blood orange or any other kind of orange
¼ cup finely chopped candied fruit
¼ cup finely chopped toasted almonds
3 tablespoons orange liqueur
¼ teaspoon vanilla extract
1 cup heavy cream, beaten
½ cup sugar
3 tablespoons light corn syrup
1 tablespoon water
6 eggs, at room temperature, well beaten

1. Brush a 6-cup **spumone** (or other ice cream) mold or round bottomed bowl well with vegetable oil.

2. Fold the rind, candied fruit, almonds, liqueur, and vanilla into the whipped cream. Place in the refrigerator.

3. In a saucepan, combine the sugar, corn syrup, and water. Cook over medium heat, stirring constantly, until sugar is completely dissolved

and mixture starts to become syrupy.

4. With an electric mixer at high speed, pour the syrup in a steady stream into the eggs, beating constantly. When all of the syrup has been incorporated, beat the mixture over ice until cold.

5. Fold the egg mixture into the chilled whipped cream and turn into the mold. Freeze overnight.

6. Unmold the **spumone** by dipping it in tepid or lukewarm water. Be very careful not to use water any hotter than tepid, as this will cause the ingredients to separate.

Note. Blood oranges are not easy to find in this country. Substitute a regular orange and blend the grated rind with 2 drops of red food coloring before adding to the whipped cream mixture.

Makes 6 servings.

Ladyfingers (Savoiardi)

This light, delicate cookie is very popular among Italian bakers. Not only is it an excellent dunking cookie, it is often used in place of a Genoa Cake or spongecake in many traditional desserts, such as **Zuppa Inglese** (page 82).

3 eggs, separated
½ cup powdered sugar, sifted
½ cup cake flour, sifted
⅛ teaspoon salt
½ teaspoon vanilla

1. Beat egg whites until stiff, gradually adding sugar.
2. In a separate bowl, beat egg yolks until thick and lemon colored. Fold into whites. Fold in sifted flour and salt. Add vanilla.

3. Cover a baking sheet with ungreased heavy paper. With a pastry bag and plain-hole tube, shape into fingers that measure about 1 x 4½ inches. Sprinkle with additional powdered sugar.

4. Bake at 350°F for 10 to 12 minutes. Remove from paper with a long spatula.

Makes 24 small cookies.

Wine Custard (Zabaglione)

This warm wine custard is indeed one of the classics. If you have a round-bottomed copper **zabaglione** pan, it can be used directly over the heat source. Otherwise, select a good-sized heavy saucepan that will fit over another pot of simmering water. Since the custard must be served immediately and is so simple to prepare, consider cooking it at the table in a **zabaglione** pan over a flame of denatured alcohol.

6 egg yolks
¼ cup sugar
½ cup Marsala wine

1. With wire whisk or electric mixer, beat together egg yolks, sugar, and wine in pan until eggs are pale and creamy.

2. Place over gently simmering, not boiling, water. Continue to beat constantly until custard stands in soft peaks when whisk or beater is withdrawn, usually about 5 minutes.

3. Spoon into champagne or other stemmed glasses, or pour into custard cups and serve immediately.

Makes 4 to 6 servings.

Variations. Substitute any one of the following wines for the Marsala—Madeira, Malvasia, Muscatel, Sauterne, or Semillon. You may choose to add a bit of anisette, cognac, rum, Amaretto, or other liqueur to the completed custard.

Cold Wine Custard (Zabaglione)

Whipping cream acts as a stabilizer for this chilled or frozen version of **zabaglione**.

4 egg yolks
¾ cup sugar
1 cup Marsala wine
½ cup dry white wine
2 tablespoons brandy
½ teaspoon salt
2 tablespoons grated lemon peel
1 tablespoon grated orange peel
2 cups heavy cream, whipped

1. Combine egg yolks with sugar in top of double boiler and beat with a wire whisk until frothy. Add Marsala, white wine, brandy, salt, and grated peel. Place over gently boiling water and

beat continuously until custard is smooth. Remove from heat and place, still in boiler top, over ice cubes in bowl to cool.

2. Whip cream and fold into cold custard with a rubber spatula. Pour into individual serving cups and freeze. Serve with fresh berries, or decorate with candied violets or glacéed fruits.

Makes about 6 servings.

Variation. Chill, but do not freeze, and serve over Poached Pears or peaches or layer in Strawberry Shortcake.

Good espresso, cappucino, *or* caffe latte *are international favorites.*

Coffee with Steamed Milk (Cappuccino)

Some home **espresso** machines have a spigot for making foamy steamed milk. But if you don't have one of these, you can purchase a small pot made expressly for milk steaming, and follow manufacturer's directions for use.

For every ¾ cup **espresso**, add 1 tablespoon or more of the foamy steamed milk. Sprinkle with cinnamon or grated dark chocolate. Add sugar to taste.

Variation. Top a cup of **espresso** with whipped cream and sprinkle with cinnamon or chocolate.

Coffee with Hot Milk (Caffè Latte)

In a large mug, combine equal parts **espresso** with milk brought just to boiling in a saucepan.

Italian Coffee (Espresso)

Italian coffee justly deserves its excellent reputation. Rich, strong *espresso* made from dark, double-roasted beans is consumed by Italians all day long.

When you purchase Italian coffee, always buy only the amount you can use in a week's time, to maintain freshness. Store in a closed jar in the refrigerator or freezer. Whole beans, ground to a fine powder for each pot of coffee, usually provide the freshest taste, although you may choose to have it ground before you take it home. Very good domestic and imported *espresso* is also available ground and packed in cans, and instant espresso powder beats its American counterpart everytime.

Authentic *espresso* can only be made in an *espresso* maker—electric or nonelectric. Use 1 coffee measure *or* 2 level tablespoons *espresso* to ¾ cup boiling water. Follow manufacturer's directions. A good substitute can easily be prepared in any slow drip coffee maker if you use finely ground *espresso* beans. After dinner *espresso* is often served with a strip of lemon peel.

After-Dinner Drinks (Liquori)

Liqueurs have long enjoyed a reputation for being medicinal, and are often credited as digestive aids. Whatever your reason for serving them, after dinner drinks (*liquori*) are a delightful end to a good meal. Serve them after or along with coffee.

There are quite a few Italian *liquori* to choose from, including Amaretto, Anisetta, Espresso Liquore, Fior d'Alpi, Galliano, Strega, Sambuca, Tears of Gold, and Tuaca.

To dramatically end your Italian dining experience, prepare a molded ice cream cassata. *Select several compatible flavors of smooth ice cream or Italian* gelati, *if available locally, or make your own favorite flavors in a home freezer. Following the shape of an ice cream mold or round-bottomed bowl, line the container with a layer of ice cream, lemon in this case, and freeze until firm. Add a layer of another flavor ice cream, again following the shape of the bowl, and freeze firmly. Continue adding as many layers and flavors as you wish until the mold is full. To unmold, dip the container briefly into warm water and invert onto a platter. Decorate with liqueur-flavored whipped cream and glaceed, dried, or fresh fruits.*

Index